The Pineapple-next-the-sea, etching 1993, **Julia Vezza**

The Pineapple, watercolour **Bob Gibson**

PINEAPPLE
RESCUED

BY THE COMMUNITY

CREAM OF LEVERTON STREET
IMPRINT

In April 1993, **Julia Vezza** etched *The Pineapple next-the-Sea* [*frontispiece*]. During a sunny afternoon session sitting outside the pub the previous summer she had overheard a conversation between visitors – 'This must be the best pub in the world.' 'The only improvement would be if there was the sea and palm trees on the other side of the road.' So she drew it.

Robert (Bob) Gibson painted the watercolour of the Pub [*second page*] for the Gately family in the early 1990s; he painted the *Pineapple diaspora* drinking in the Jorene Celeste (the Oxford), *page 158*, for the drinkers.

Ken Pyne painted several large posters for *St Patrick's Night* during the Gately era [*page 36*]; they all adorned the bar/darts area every 17 March – when Guinness was £1.50 a pint, double whiskey £2. On occasions, Ken's cartoons for the *Evening Standard* and the *Ham & High* featured the Pineapple.

Evening Standard: 07.01.02 **Ken Pyne**

Maps [*page 6*] amalgamated from [top] part of Ordnance Survey London Sheet III 92, 1869 and [bottom] part of London Sheet XVI 2, 1870 (with permission of Camden Local Studies and Archives Centre).

The *back cover* shares words (written by Martin James) with the plaque commemorating The Pineapple War 2001–2002 presented by Kirk McGrath and Paul Davies 07.12.2007 following their purchase of the pub and hung in the corridor behind the bar.

IT WAS WORTH IT SO WE FOUGHT FOR IT

On 6 December 2001 the regulars in the Pineapple might not have said they had the *'best pub in the world'* or the *'perfect pub'*; but on that day a developer prepared to take it away from us. The primeval instinct, to stop 'someone' taking away a most precious asset, led to a stalwart defence of *'our pub'*.

This is not a record of the hours, days and months leading to the sale of the pub we did not know we would ever have to 'save'. It is a beer-stained tribute to friendship generated in and around the Pineapple.

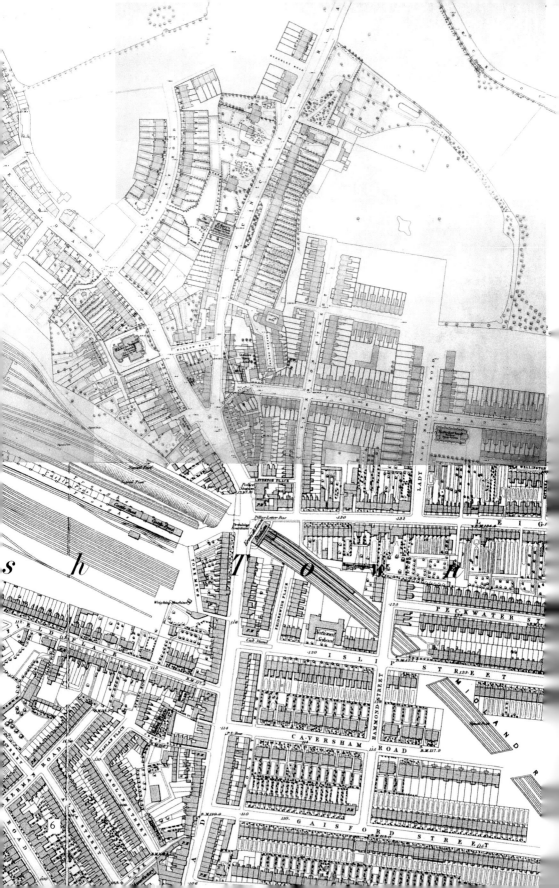

1868 saw the arrival of the Midland Railways in Kentish Town and the opening of the terminus at St Pancras. The railway brought the decimation of large areas of land and housing on either side of Kentish Town Road and north of the Euston Road at King's Cross. New housing in Kentish Town spread into the grounds of St John's College Park; the Georgian cul-de-sac of Leverton Street was extended in small sections over the next fifteen years providing homes for workers in the fast-growing city including the new railwaymen. The Pineapple was part of this new build; a small pub hidden amongst the housing on a cross-roads on which four shops were added – a baker, grocer and milkman, a greengrocer and a general store also selling oil. The pub never had a fascia sign; its name is in its exterior decoration sporting pineapples above every window and doorway. With a simple interior shape, it had three entrances, an outside gents', a kitchen with range on the lower ground floor, a cellar the width of the building, a first floor function room and accommodation on the second floor. The grandeur was in the bar-back – mahogany with panels advertising brandies, whiskies and wines in gold leaf and painted glass and two large mirrors etched with pineapples – a huge investment for its builder-owner. The local competition on the side streets would have come from the equally new Falkland (built late 1869); on the high street the Bull and Gate and the Assembly House, already in its second existence, were overtaken by decay. The Bull and Gate was rebuilt in 1871 and the Assembly eventually re-appeared as a 'palace' in 1898.

The railway brought Bass from Burton-on Trent distributed from new cellars beneath St Pancras Station. The brewery would eventually provide the pub with very large and expensive made-to-measure advertising mirrors over each fireplace (1870s). The railway also brought an off-loading place for cattle that were then walked along Leighton Road on the way to Market Road. The Pineapple cellars were used by butchers.

The addition of inside toilets was the only change to the building in 133 years. The off-sales between the two bars was probably created in the 1940s and lost in the late 1970s; the Double Diamond windows were probably put in during the 1950s. The piano in the public bar lasted until the 80s; there were resident piano players but customers played too – Jack Straw played after Labour Party meetings in the early 80s.

1868

Pineapple publicans

John Wakelin	1868–1871
Alfred Smith	1871–1876
William Poyser	1877–1878
Henry Wakely	1878–1880
William Leahy	1880–1890
John Jones	1890–1892
Thomas George Walker	1892–1902
William Gimlett	1902–1908
Charles Daniel Hawkin	1908–1912
William Alfred Carter	1912–1914
George Norris Carter	1914–1915
Elizabeth Champ	1915–1916
Louisa Mary Balsdon	1916–1917
Edward Frank Harvey	1917–1930
Francis Hefworth	1930–1934
William Albert Wicks	1934–1935
William Arthur Eyre	1935–1938
Joseph George Spencer	1938–1950
Thomas R Errington	1950–1958
Arthur M Pike	1958–1964
George & Phyllis(Phoebe) Brady	1964–1976
John & Patricia Phillips	1976–1985
James & Mary Gordon	1985–1987
Seán & Mary Gately	1987–1992
Christine, Seán & Mary Gately	1992–2001

drinking years 133

Francis and Chloe Powell	2002 – 2007
Paul Davies and Kirk McGrath	2007–

8 **VE Day** 1945: the Pineapple is the focus of attention

Pineapple memories on tap

THE troubled times for regulars of the Pineapple in Kentish Town were happily unknown when this snap was taken several years ago.

No talk of takeovers, luxury flats or property development in those days.

Highlights of the week then were darts competitions, charity suppers, and organising the next beano. Occasionally, the gossip of the area found itself in these columns.

The smiling folks pictured, including licensee Phyllis, were dressed up for a Cockney night out.

10   **George and Phoebe Brady,** landlords 1964 – 1976

Since 1868, landlords had provided the local community with a centre for recreation. In 2001 local memories went back through five families of landlords, and men and women in their fifties and sixties told tales of their parents and grandparents drinking, playing and celebrating in the Pineapple.

Gus's band of **pigeon fanciers** and their wives met on Sunday lunchtimes (the **Broken wing club?**). It is whispered that one of Gus's pigeons received a medal for life-saving action with the 8th Army in North Africa during World War II; Gus did receive medals for his work in the service. *MC*

In its prime the **Gentlemen's walking club** met once every four or six weeks. *Gentlemen* would meet at the Pineapple dressed in tweeds, strong boots, hats with feathers (Tyrolean type), with a variety of canes and walking sticks. They would then 'straggle' to a declared destination, a pub within a three-mile radius, drink would be taken and the return trip made in time for last orders. Simple pleasures in the name of exercise! *MH*

In the 1980s the function room was the venue, every two or three months, for **poetry nights**; people reading their own work or that of others. Nights of laughter and tears. *MH*

Pensioners' Christmas lunch: In the days of Phoebe and George [land-lords], a Christmas lunch was cooked in the flat upstairs and the kitchens of neighbours; it was served in the function room by bar staff and locals to all of the local pensioners. Those that had difficulty getting to the pub were fetched and taken home. *MH, EI*

Four-pub pram race – teams represented four local pubs – the Falkland, Gloucester, Assembly and Pineapple. The annual race was a high speed circuit by each 'mum' and 'baby'-laden pram to each of the pubs, in turn, downing a pint in each of the four pubs on arrival. No real babies, many broken axles, many pints.

The pub seems to have always encouraged ***dressing-up nights***; Tramps, Roaring 20s, Vicars and tarts, Topsy-turvy and Cockney nights were regular features in the 60s, 70s and 80s.

Phoebe and George started the **Easter bonnet competitions**; and organised **day trips** to the coast by coach in summer.

Flo Chesnais (1918–97), mother of Mandy Callender, moved in 1957 to 45 Montpelier Grove; with two young daughters, and another on the way, she took jobs in the early morning and evenings. She was a cleaner at the Pineapple (and Falkland) and helped out behind the (Pineapple) bar. Flo was regarded as a pillar of the local community; Mandy recalls having to regularly give up her room to student guests without a bed. Flo was key in all social events; in the photographs, *pages 12–25*, you will find her serving at the eel stall, in all the dressing-up nights and Easter bonnet competitions. She was captain of the ladies' darts team and co-opted by the men's team when they were short of players. *MC*

top left: roaring 20s

top centre: tramps' night, sausages cooked on a primus stove, money collected for orphanage

top right: Falkland Queen is crowned by local
Cllr Sally Peltier 1978

Cockney night [1969] was accompanied by an eel stall outside   13

14   Flo shows off her hairy chest (wig) outside the gents in the saloon bar

16   Flo and Edi: Easter bonnet competition March 1964

18   *top:* Easter bonnets 1964 [winner Flo, fifth from left]

top: Easter bonnets 1965 [winner Mum, front row second right]   19

20   Summer trip to Margate (or Southend) 1964 (or 65)!

(imagine getting a driver to reverse into Railey Mews today!)   21

22   Women's darts outings; *bottom left* to Southend 1970. Flo captain.

Pineapple team: 1 Mandy Callender, 2 Flo Chesnais (Mandy's Mum), 3 Phoebe Brady (landlady 1964-76),
4 Pat Phillips (landlady 1976-85), 5 Sandra Grant, 6 Jean Philips, 7 Maggie Cooney, 8 Terry Cooney.
Journalists: *named in chalk* Dave, Jean, Kit, Adrian, John D, Pete, Howard

Pineapple darts team vs *Camden Journal* 1981 [during the journalists' strike]   23

The three door entrance from Leverton Street, public, off sales, and saloon bar often features

top 'Mum', Vi (barmaid), Mandy and Flo (Mandy's mother) "obviously an occasion, there's a sweet sherry"

Two generations of Hanlons and four generations of Quintons inside and outside the pub   25

Opening night of the Gately era...

When we took on the Pineapple there was really only one room to live in. There was no real kitchen, and no bathroom. Matty came over to help, moved in, and got pneumonia. The family moved in, to a shambles, in January 1987. The heating did not get sorted for months; at the end of an evening we used to warm ourselves up in the bar with a couple of large brandies while the electric blanket warmed up the bed and then we'd fly into it.

The opening night at the Pineapple was a truly memorable occasion. The old crowd from the Woodman turned up, of course, as well as the regular crowd from the Pineapple. A massive fight broke out between these two contingents in the Public Bar.
Mary G

2001

NW5: KENTISH TOWN

Pineapple
51 Leverton Street
☎ (020) 7209 4961
12 (11 Sat)-11; 12-10.30 Sun
Boddingtons Bitter; Brakspear Bitter; Marston's Pedigree Ⓗ
Unchanging, family-run, cosy, back-street oasis with a loyal following.
≹ ⊖ ♣

NW8: ST JOHNS WOOD

FOR MARY!

OCT '93. KENTISHTOWN.

28 Photo of Mary Gately taken by a German student 1993

FOR CHRISTINE!   OCT '93 · KENTISH TOWN

Photo of Christine Gately taken by a German student 1993   29

Bollards

At one time the council, in their wisdom, put a bollard on the pavement outside the Pineapple, ostensibly to prevent cars parking too close. It never had this effect, but the post stayed. This always hindered the deliveries, and one delivery truck did knock it over, not entirely, but noticeably. When the council returned to do another job, as they seem to do every year, a 32-ton dumper truck with hydraulic lifting gear was used to clear the rubble. Seán was sitting outside the pub at the time with his paper, and when the dumper driver had finished his job, Seán nodded at him, nodded at the post: "Could you take it with you?" "Sure" said the bloke (an Irishman, of course) and hoisted the bollard straight into his truck. Seán concluded the deal with "will you have a drink?" "I'll have a pint of lager". The two men hadn't met before, but soon established that they came from the same part of Ireland and had friends in common. An hour or so, and three pints later, Seán's new friend drove off with the bollard. *Mary G*

The Stella champions

One year, Seán and Tony went to the Stella Artois tennis championships at Queen's Club. Seán had persuaded a rep to give him two free passes for men's finals day. Tony and Seán went off in a cab.

As Tony describes it, 'there was a huge marquee, with a massive bar where you could have anything to drink you wanted. We started on the Pimms. Tables for eight were laid out around the enormous space. We got a four-course meal, we got wine, brandy and cigars, and half-way through the meal the Stella bigwig on our table started to give out match tickets. When we finally stood up from the meal, Seán asked "Will you watch the tennis then?" "Don't mind"'.

So they went outside, gave away their match tickets, and went back into the marquee to resume their consumption of Pimms, which they continued to do until they were thrown out at about 8pm. They never saw a game, they never saw a player...

...then it was a cab back to the Pineapple. *Tony D*

Pineapple's own stars...

A Pineappler [GO] hired the Holyhead–Dun Laoghaire Ferry for a day trip on Wednesday 29 July 1981, the wedding day of Charles and Diana; when interviewed by a BBC Radio reporter he growled "Llewelyn is the only Prince of Wales". 750 Welsh people 'celebrated' with him including one from the *Welsh Embassy* who recalls helping to drink the boat, and some Irish pubs, dry and nothing about Dublin. The BBC replayed the interview on the day of Charles's second marriage. *GO/DM*

...and the Pineappler who was Crew Commander of a Green Goddess during the national Firemen's strike [1977] – called to rescue a cat from a tree; collects cat, hands cat to the owner, cat runs away – the Green Goddess drives off – over the cat. *Mike B [EI recalls: The story was relayed on ITV News by Reggie Bosanquet, who was nearly sacked because he couldn't stop himself laughing].*

The side door

About 20 years ago [1990] I had arranged to meet a man called Martin at 12:30 in the Pineapple (Martin was not a secret lover, but Camden's new art inspector for whom I had been doing some work, and who had taken me to lunch; this was to be on me). I got to the Pineapple at noon (wanting to be settled, with drink in, in case Martin was early) only to find it locked, barred and bolted. HELP.

I was seen lurking by Seán when he came outside for some reason. 'Sorry, we don't open until 1 o'clock.' 'Oh hell!' I said and explained my predicament. Furtively, Seán guided me to the side door. 'You don't have a problem'. He poured me a cider and said he had to be off for a bit, but to help myself if I wanted more. So I made myself at home and read my book in the empty and slightly spooky Pineapple.

As it was, the man Martin was late, opening time became official – and the pub unlocked, unbarred and unbolted by the time he appeared. I'd had two more ciders and was feeling very pampered, mellow and merry. We drank into the afternoon (AND I got some more work). *Julia V*

Snaffled by dog...

The family were upstairs. We heard Kim and Phil 'arrive' at the pub, heard the dropping of shopping, the rush to the bar, the clacking of optics being furiously worked. Then peace and calm – shattered by a sudden shriek. As the new arrivals had put their shopping down, it had tumbled all over the floor. Seeing a nice, large, fresh French stick, Sandy [the pub dog] had assumed it must be Sunday breakfast, and had consumed more than half of it by the time they looked up. Kim was not amused, especially as she had to go back down the High Street for the replacement. *Christine G*

Dog snaffled...

Having left Paddy outside Mary G was waiting for a prescription at the chemist in Fortess Road when a bloke walking by untied the dog and set off towards Tufnell Park. Finding the dog missing Mary returned distraught to the pub; Christine phoned customers and staff likely to be at home. Pat 'Nice', on the look-out for the dog, found Paddy and his new minder sitting in a queue at a 134 bus stop. Deciding on an Exocet approach to the 'unsteady' man, without introduction she prised open the 'filthy' fingers gripping the lead: 'That's my dog and I am going to take him'. The bemused, speechless, rough sleeper stood staring at his empty hand as the spaniel was marched away down the road; the dog remained completely unfazed while admonished as 'YOU TART' all the way back to Leverton Street. [A medal was struck on 28.01.98] *Pat P*

Paddy's Night rescue...

So it was St Patrick's Night, must be something like 20 years or so ago [pre-1989]. Nobody can quite remember, but Nick and Ali were living in Dunollie Place at the time, which means it was some time back. Long before the end of the celebrations in the Pineapple, which consisted of the usual OTT quantities of drink being taken (it is believed Father Chris was in the pub that night!) Ali had already staggered off home in search of the horizontal, leaving Nick to carry on the good fight.

At the end of the proceedings Seán and Mary had retired upstairs for a well-earned rest and they just happened to look out of the living room window, whereupon they spied a prostrate Nick, lying completely sparko in the lee of a handy skip parked in Ascham Street. The hour was very late and it was also raining gently, so Seán decided that the Good Samaritan hat was required and headed off back downstairs. He went out and when he got to Nick prodded him on the sole of his boot, enquiring whether he was of a mind to be going home any time soon. Nick cracked open one eye and replied that he was thinking about it. However, there was no sign of further movement. Having no alternative, and doubtless heaving a heavy sigh, Seán got a hold of the boy, hauled him to his feet leaving a star-shaped dry shadow where he had lain, and began the long and tortuously weaving journey to Chez Hinton/Watt. It is not known how long it took for Ali to open the door to the pair, but Seán was gone an hour or so on his good deed. It is also a matter of conjecture as to her state of dress when she did so, but for years afterward it pleased Seán to tease her about the "Emerald in her belly button".

All in all a sterling act of kindness, and one that not many landlords would be prepared to undertake. *AW*

New Year's Eve rescue...

Once upon a time... Mike Jones had a rented room at The Junction. Following 'the usual OTT quantities of drink being taken' Mike rang for a mini-cab to get him home and when asked gave his home telephone number. The cab had not arrived an hour later; it being 5:00am Seán and Mary wanted to lock up. Mike left weaving his way up the hill and with some difficulty got in to The Junction. He was woken by the phone. 'Your cab is outside the Pineapple Mr Jones'.

Mike dressed and walked back to Leverton Street to take the cab home to the Junction.

After hours

The vacuum was certainly being pushed across the pile between the tables with enthusiasm and the musical hummmming from the operative was definitely audible above the chatter; John C, still drinking-up, asked John 'the Hoover' if he was happy or just trying to disguise the fact that the Hoover had packed up? Caught in the arc lights he stopped, grinned, shrugged his shoulders and leant down and switched it on. *John C*

(Pine)apple of the locals' eyes

The Pineapple

Leverton Street, NW5
0171-485 6422.

THE PEN may be mightier than the sword, but a shotgun with its barrels lovingly trimmed by an accomplished bank robber is a very different matter indeed.

It is a stroke of luck then that the novelists, actors and armed robbers who populate Kentish Town in roughly equal numbers seem to manage to live together in apparent harmony.

The literary-leaning inhabitants even have what appears to be their own local, The Pineapple in Leverton Street, and a very agreeable watering hole it is too.

The outside of the pub, which features prominently in at least one recently published novel, Emma Daily's Tomorrow's Past, has even been thoughtfully emblazoned with pineapples to ensure even the most observationally-challenged drinking partner can find it.

Through the doors, and the thick curtain that ensures added cosiness on a freezing night, a knot of regulars surround the bar, while other drinkers congregate at tables around two fireplaces.

The welcome from behind the bar is friendly and there is no sneer even if you choose a soft drink instead of something a bit stronger to keep out the chill.

The beers are well selected – Stella Artois, Guinness, Marston's Pedigree, Greene King IPA and Boddingtons – and well-kept. The Stella is cool and crisp, the Guinness admirable and the Pedigree not bad at all. For novelty seekers there are also some imaginative bottled beers and alcoholic sodas.

Sinking into the plush red upholstery, drinkers can enjoy their own conversations or eavesdrop comfortably on the pleasant drone of others. The jukebox is pitched as, very definitely, background noise.

Live music is performed on some evenings, but consists of nothing more disturbing than gentle, folky strings played by affable hippy-types.

The residents of Leverton Street have a great little local, so it's not suprising the landlady is a bit taken aback when fitness fiends ring up and enquire whether it is a dance studio.

MALCOLM JONES

● The Pineapple in Leverton Street: definitely *not* a dance studio.

1999

NW5: KENTISH TOWN

PINEAPPLE
51 Leverton St ☎ (0171) 209 4961
12.30-11; 12-10.30 Sun
Greene King IPA; Marston's
Pedigree; Theakston Best
Bitter Ⓗ

Cosy, Victorian back-street local with a loyal following. Occasional quiz nights and banjo music. Note the magnificent Bass brewery mirror above the fireplace.
≠ ⊖ ♣

The pub's first entry in the CAMRA Good Beer Guide was 1980 [when locals probably did not care] then each year between 1980-1985 and 1990-2001.

2001

Pineapple
51 Leverton Street, NW5 (020 7485 6422).
Kentish Town tube/rail. **Open** 3-11pm Mon-Fri;
noon-11pm Sat; noon-10.30pm Sun. **No credit cards**
With flowery wallpaper, deep carpets, fresh flowers and fireplaces around its cramped little bar, the Pineapple feels like a rather chintzy hidden drinking den, an impression accentuated and its location sitting on a corner by a cobbled mews in a residential street. Furthermore, you have to push through heavy curtains as you make your way through the front door, and then in the evenings you may have to squeeze in further between the very mixed and friendly crowd of punters. There are as many women as men who frequently fill the place here, gathered around the TV or chatting at tables at the other end. It sticks to what it's best at – no food of any kind, and a regular list of just three bitters (Pedigree, Brakspear, Boddingtons all £2.10), but they're expertly kept, which has made it a favourite among beer aficionados. There's also a good range of lagers on tap (around the £2.20 mark) and an enjoyable wine selection. One final touch of character is provided by the perkily painted pineapples, which were somehow built into the pub's original Victorian exterior.
Babies and children admitted. Disabled: toilet. Games
(darts room). Quiz (monthly, check with pub). Satellite TV.
Tables outdoors (pavement).

The pub's press cuttings   33

The Pineapple *Kentish Town London*

Pineapple Social Club
Newsletter No. 1
Jan-March 1996

This is the first of the quarterly newsletters for the Pineapple Social Club. This year we are hoping to keep you up-to-date with all the news and information of events and outings each quarter, so that you can keep the dates free in your diary and encourage your nearest and dearest to let their hair down in the company of some of North London's finest drinkers.

Events January- March

1) Double Darts Knockout Match: Thursday, January 25th
   Entry fee: £1.50, partners chosen by draw, Cash Prizes *(orgs: Kate and Mike Bobb)*

2) St Valentine's Night Quiz: Wednesday, February 14th
   Life, love and other things – BIG questions and CASH prizes *(orgs: Imogen and Simon Holmes)*

3) Dog Racing Evening: Saturday, February 24th   £22 —
   Back the right bow-wow and find Pineapple Pals for Life... *(orgs: Imogen and Simon Holmes)*

   Coach.
   Admission
   Programme
   2 course
   Dinner

4) Competition Crib Night: Thursday, March 7th
   Entry fee: £1.00, Cash Prizes *(orgs: n.a.a.)*

5) St Patrick's Night Super Raffle: Sunday, March 17th
   The regular Pineapple Jamboree for the Patron Saint of Gately's *(org: Christine Gately)*

6) Bowling Evening: Wednesday, March 27th
   Bowling at North London's hot-shot alley in Finsbury Park *(org: Christine Gately)*
   PLUS: four raffles each month - with booze prizes, and extra prizes on quiz nights.

(Bank Holiday W/End) → Sat 4 - Tues 7 May £235-50
Events later in the year:

A quick overview of some of the events later in the year: *Direct Flight*
There are four more QUIZ NIGHTS to come: Easter; Midsummer; Halloween and   *Galway*
Christmas. The TRIP TO GALWAY will take place over May Bank Holiday (May 4-6th)   *Tax*
(see Christine). A supermarket smash'n grab TRIP TO FRANCE (Boulogne) is planned in
early November, leaving on a Saturday and returning on a Sunday. Sarah Rutry or Sarah 4 ×
Cooper can be contacted with any HELPFUL ideas or advice you have on the subject. The *Hotel.*
next newsletter will be out in March with the breathtaking Spring timetable of events.

If you have any further suggestions or requests, please contact Christine or any of the usual suspects mentioned above.

On a practical note, SUBS will be collected every month, by either Chris Gately or Sarah Cooper; minimum payment is £5.00. If subscriptions lapse for more than two months, the amount already saved will be returned, without profit, and club membership curtailed for the year. You have been warned! This year the club's charity donation will be made to the homeless, through a local church.

Trip to the races at Sandown   35

ST PATRICK'S NIGHT

SATURDAY **17** MARCH

GUINNESS £1.50
IRISH WHISKEY DOUBLE £2

DOGS
WALTHAMSTOW
SATURDAY
21
NOVEMBER
5:30
MEET HERE
PINEAPPLE
NAMES TO CHRISTINE OR MIKE

KNOCK-OUT
DARTS
THURSDAY
16
DECEMBER
8:00
CASH PRIZES
£1 ENTRY
PINEAPPLE

CHRISTMAS
QUIZ PINEAPPLE
THURSDAY
10
DECEMBER
8:00

CASH PRIZES
£1 ENTRY
MAXIMUM FOUR TO A TEAM

KARTING

PINEAPPLE

SATURDAY

15

APRIL

09:00-12:00

15 PLACES

NAMES TO CHRISTINE OR MIKE

TEN-PIN BOWLING

FRIDAY

30

MARCH

7:15

MEET HERE

PINEAPPLE

NAMES TO MIKE OR TO BAR STAFF

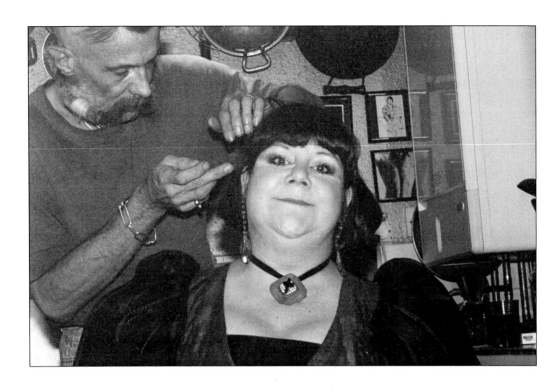

The Pineapple had always served as a meeting place, a local forum, and a source of community news and activity. It was the place to find out who is ill, or short of cash, or looking for a job, or in any way in need of assistance – a visit, food, money; to find a tradesman, a place for your spare keys, a place to find someone to 'get into' your house. A place for celebration and commiseration, the venue for birthday parties, christenings and wakes; the whole pub going to weddings and funerals. The place where differentiation may well be by job 'title': John 'the Hoover', John 'Wormald', 'Portuguese' Pete, 'banjo' Pete, 'the hat', 'the grin', and surnames never known. The place where sport was watched together; allegiances were noted, Blackburn, Tranmere, Norwich, Middlesbrough, Leicester, alongside the London separations between QPR, Chelsea, Spurs, Arsenal, Millwall [and ManU]. Where national loyalties were exposed in rugby, cricket and football and where 40 people who left work early on a Monday [1997], gathered to watch the 4.00pm start of the postponed Grand National.

Fundraising events included darts, quizzes [when quizzes were for kudos and raising money] and raffles for national and local issues: a darts match between the Pineapple and *The Camden Journal* to raise funds for striking journalists at the newspaper; a quiz and raffle to raise funds for the rebuilding of a school for handicapped children [in North Essex] destroyed by fire, attended by a friend's child; a quiz and raffle to raise funds for Great Ormond Street Hospital, Wishing Well Appeal [1987], to redevelop the hospital and build parental accommodation. Simon was a cricketer in the film *Lagaan* [2000–1] in Gujarat state in western India; an earthquake devastated this region and displaced many locals. The crew contributed monetarily to the rebuilding and the Pineapple raised the money for two houses.

And **laugh together** …did you hear about the Pineappler who was accidentally locked in the *24 hour shop* overnight [because it did not operate 24 hrs] while shopping for his supper after closing time. In an effort to prove that nothing had, or would be, stolen the legally aware shopper sat on the floor under the gaze of the security camera; a night spent dozing and waking to the relentless pulse of chiller motors and the swirling cold draughts. Having just 'dropped off' when the door shutter was raised and the newspapers thrown in at 05.00 another two hours of sleepless incarceration were to pass before the shopkeepers arrived. Challenging their contention that a burglar had been caught with an angry retort about 'damages for false imprisonment' he tossed his coin across the counter and left with his tin of stew. There was no film in the camera.

…and were you there when MB, returning from Switzerland arm in a sling having had a collision with a moving vehicle, came through the red velvet curtain to be greeted by a cheery Des: "…hello Michael, you look a little run down".

48   Party at someone else's home, garden; lunch with *the ladies who lunch*

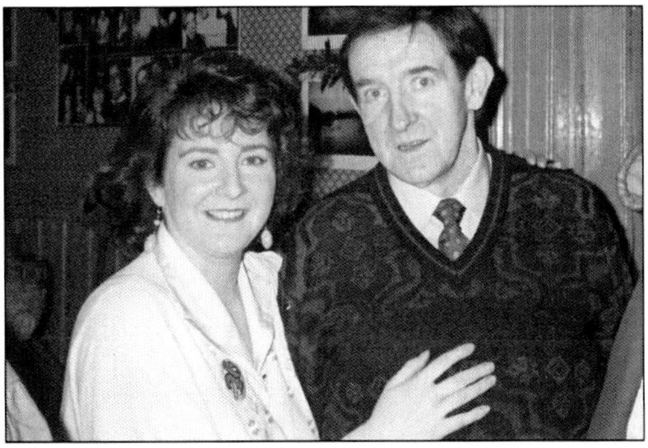

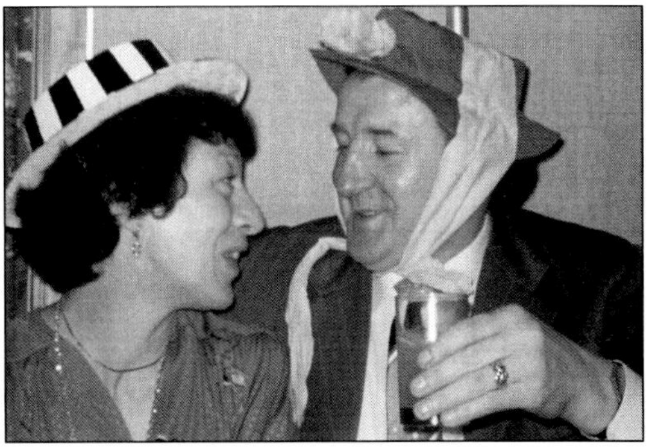

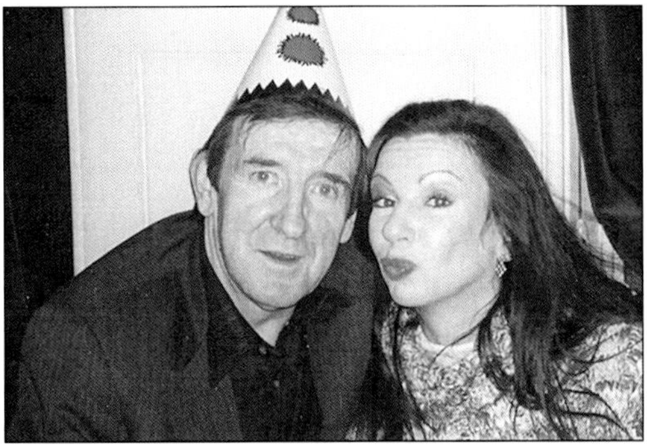

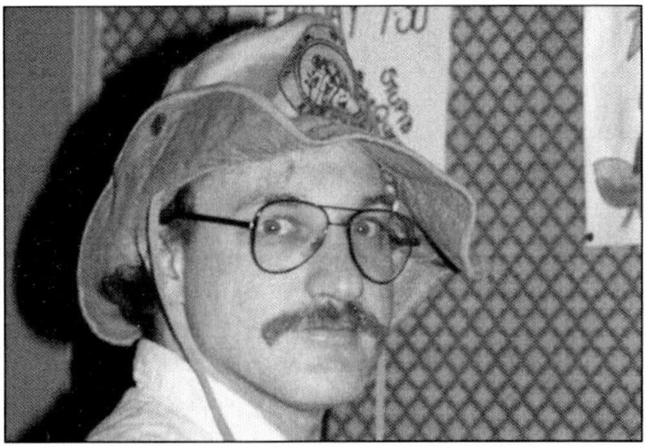

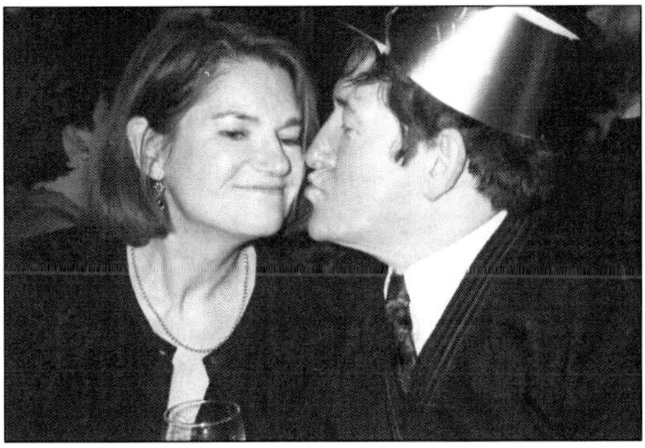

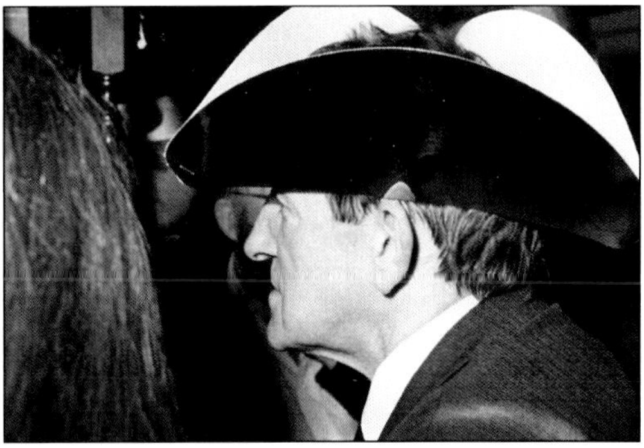

...any excuse to dress-up or wear a hat

52   A place for keys, camaraderie

Hello Brian Williams, have you been to the bank? Play you for £2? £3? Go on! Go on! OK, 50p. *BW*

Card sharp Newly moved to the neighbourhood, and dressed like Omar Sharif, Wynne was made very welcome on his first visit to the Pub. Seán whispered to Mary "He looks like a card player." "Actually, no I'm not," said the alert Wynne "best decision I ever made!" *WT*

Once in a life time "I got him for £400 one Sunday playing shoot pontoon. I came in on Monday and he ignored me. It took me till Thursday week to get my money." "Was it the only time you won?" "Nooo, but probably overall I lost a fortune. Course he drank water". *DM*

The reckoning Seán had died. Mogsi went to pay his respects at Levertons. Back in the Pineapple, with Mary behind the bar, he started to cry. Mary to Mogsi "I don't know why you are so upset, you still owe Seán £20 from cards." *DM*

Website Address: http://www.camden.gov.uk/planning
Email Address: env.devcon@camden.gov.uk

ENVIRONMENT

Development Control
Planning Services
London Borough of Camden
Town Hall
Argyle Street
London WC1H 8ND

Tel 020 7278 4444
Fax 020 7974 1975

TOWN AND COUNTRY PLANNING ACT 1990

NOTICE OF RECEIPT OF A PLANNING APPLICATION

Date of Notice: 10 -12- 01

ADDRESS: 51 Leverton Street NW5

PROPOSAL:
Change of use of former pub building with roof extension, to
provide 3x maisonettes & 1x flat.
New structure at rear facing Railey Mews being a B1 office
unit with parking space,
(Plans Submitted)

Application number: PEX0100941/
Associated number :

You can look at the application and any submitted plans at the One
Stop Reception on the 5th Floor of Camden Town Hall, Argyle Street,
WC1 8EQ. The Reception is open between 9.00am and 5.00pm, Monday to
Friday, with extended opening till 7.00pm on Thursdays. A duty
planner is available during these times to assist you in looking at
plans and to offer general planning advice. Plans are also
available on the Council's website at Camden.gov.uk/planning.

If you would like to submit comments on the application, please do
so, in writing or by email, within 21 days of the date on this
notice. (Please quote the application number)

NOTIFICATION OF COMMITTEE DATE
If the decision is to be taken by the Development Control Sub-
Committee we will tell you the date of the committee if you clearly
ask us to in your letter.

Please also note that the proposal described above may not cover
all aspects of the application. The submitted plans may show
additional information.

The application is being dealt with by **John Davies** on **020 7974
5885.**

Director of Environment Department

NOT1letter.

INVESTOR IN PEOPLE

Director Peter Bishop

Nightmare on Leverton Street

Michael Balfour found during the afternoon of 6 December 2001, attached to the lamp-post outside the pub, a planning notice *for change of use of a **former** pub building with roof extension, to provide 1x flat and 3x maisonettes plus B1 office unit with parking space in Railey Mews*. It was dated 7 December. He removed it, made copies and distributed them in the pub that evening. Planning permission had been applied for by a developer who did not own the building. The pub was to close on 16 December; completion was set for 21 December.

10 days until the pub closed!
14 days until the developer owned the pub.
21 days to object to the planning application.
Don't panic!

06.12.01

Shock and awe spreads around the bar; Friday 7 December

Crown, Prince of Wales Road *converted (flats)*
Dreghorn Castle, Queens Crescent *converted (betting shop)*
Carlton, Weedington Road *converted (flats)*
Malden Arms, Malden Road *converted (flats)*
Newberry, Malden Road *demolished*
Harmood, Harmood Road *converted (flats)*
Load of Hay, Haverstock Hill *squatted, returned as bar-restaurant*
Falkland, Falkland Road *converted (flats)*
White Rose of England, Talacre Road *demolished*
Torriano, Leighton Road *closed, returned as bar*
Admiral Napier, Warden Road *converted (flats)*
Crimea, Inkerman Road *converted (flats)*
Duke of Cambridge, Lawford Road *converted (flats)*
Jolly Anglers Arms, Kentish Town Road *converted (restaurant)*

14

pubs lost in Kentish Town
in the **five years** up to 2001

According to CAMRA, 380 pubs were lost between 2000 and the beginning of 2002, almost all, in the era of *development opportunity,* being turned into housing. A developer had got *our pub.* And we had found out after exchange of contracts.

We did not want to lose our pub. We did not drink in a dying pub. We had no intention of being another statistic. We all knew what we had, we knew every way in which the pub was special; the people, the amenity, the fabric.

We knew we would have to consider anything and everything *to stop* the developer. From day one we knew only a listing would stop the destruction of the building. A photocopy (of the office copy) of the English Heritage booklet *Pubs, understanding listing* was delivered by an officer on his way home past the pub. We had guidance but no guarantee of a listing for a back street local and little time.

380
UK pubs lost to developers in two years

Application for spot listing

Pineapple public house
51 Leverton Street
London NW5 2NX

Built 1868

" THE CREAM OF
LEVERTON STREET "
[PINEAPPLE]

Sale of this property goes through on 21 December 2001.
Closing date for comments on the
Application for planning permission 28 December 2001.
The public house closes on Sunday 16 December 2001
to enable the present occupants to move out.

We have four days to get the organisation in to see the very fine back bar
between 3.00pm and 11.00pm daily. We may get permission from the owners to view
at other times and next week but we cannot be sure.

We are most concerned that the new owners do not damage the back bar behind
closed doors once the sale is completed on 21 December 2001.

The exterior facades of this corner building are good examples of a back street
local Victorian public house built as the street was built in 1867-68.
It has not been modified.

The public bar retains many of its original features but the back bar is unique and
a very fine example. It was built for this pub and contains fine examples of etched
mirror work and gold foil inlay letters and decorations. The wood surround and
the carved capitals are also complete.

- 8 photographs of the back bar are attached.
  (6 sheets of exterior images, to supplement those already submitted)
- Copy of Application for planning
- Site map

Contact:
Gill Scott
48 Rochester Place
London NW1 9JX

phone 0207 267 7016
fax 0207 284 1556
studio@gillscott-design.co.uk

PINEAPPLE
51 Leverton Street, NW5 2NX

Street facade
1 Both street facades retain all original features and decoration.
Ground floor plan
2 Open floor plan is original; no changes to arches or to ceiling coving.
3 Richly detailed back-bar. Mahogany woodwork, gold-painted capitals
   carved pineapple references at bar counter level;
   signs, etched, painted and gold-leafed;
   mirrors with pineapple references, etched, engraved and painted;
   infill pannels, etched, engraved, painted and gold-leafed.
4 Original fire place. Mirror over – S Trenner & Son, Gray's Inn Road, WC
5 Original stair case. Cast-iron newel post has pineapple references.

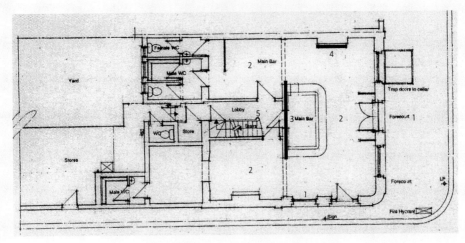

Cellar floor plan evidence of premises being occupied
by butchers pre 1868. *Unable to find a brick with carved date 1852
mentioned in news paper article 1970's held in Camden archives.*
6 White ceramic tiles pre 1867 probably 1850's.
7 Kitchen range
8 Wall paper, two layers – first printed wood, second decorative pattern
   probably 1860's.
9 Butchers hanging rails (in ceiling).
10 Original stair case.

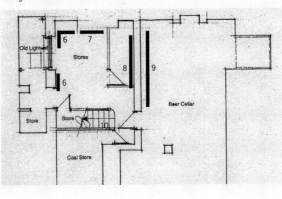

CLOSING
16 DECEMBER

"THE CREAM OF LEVERTON STREET"
PINEAPPLE
WHERE NOTHING MAKES SENSE
ANY MORE

REOPENING
AS FLATS

**HELP <u>STOP</u> THE CHANGE OF USE.
RESCUE YOUR LOCAL**

Eleven locals met for the first time as a *committee* on the evening of 7 December. The word had to get out beyond the pub and very quickly. Publicity was needed.

Press releases went to national and local papers; stars of film and TV who normally drank anonymously in the pub offered themselves for a photo shoot. The voices of locals were heard in interview on local and national radio.

We needed the neighbourhood to know about the planning application: a banner for the pub, posters for Mehmet's [the local corner shop], window posters for local residents. We needed to inform the neighbourhood of the implications of the planning application and the urgent timescale: flyers went into the newspapers sold from Mehmet's, 450 more were delivered within two days. We hoped the neighbour-hood would respond by writing to the Council. A small group, including planners and lawyers, started analysing Camden's planning documents to find reasons to reject the plans for housing and offices and to submit a formal response.

In the same week the Government Department of Culture, Media and Sport was quoted in the national newspapers: 'the community value of an old building can be a critical factor in deciding whether it is kept'; we decide to prove it.

NEWS

London mayor and poet laureate among campaigners

Ken and chums join battle to save pub

by DAN CARRIER

AN AWARD-winning Kentish Town pub is fighting for its life after property developers have earmarked it for a yuppie-style flats development.

The Pineapple, named by the Campaign for Real Ale as one of north London's finest pubs, has been bought by property developers following the death of its landlord in October.

It was sold by the landlord's family with the understanding that the pub – which is still a viable business – would be kept open while the upper floors were renovated. But just days after the contract was signed the developers made a fresh application to Camden Council to turn the whole building in to maisonettes and put in a two-storey office at the back of the pub.

Regulars have started a campaign to preserve their watering hole. Supporters of the pub include London mayor Ken Livingstone, filmmaker Ken Loach, broadcaster Jon Snow, the poet laureate Andrew Motion and actor Rufus Sewell.

Ken Livingstone told the New Journal: "Local facilities, including places to relax and socialise, are vital to provide a sense of community. It seems to me that the Pineapple is the sort of local pub that is all too often disappearing in London."

He commented: "The Pineapple represents the kind of pub that is falling victim to rising house prices that attract speculators. It should be left well

Jonty Boyce, a regular at the award-winning pub, who is co-ordinating a campaign to save it from being turned into yuppie flats

alone." Last orders will be called on Sunday December 16 – weeks before its future has been decided by the council.

Jonty Boyce, a regular who is helping co-ordinate the campaign to save the pub, told the New Journal locals would not let it disappear. He said: "It is one of the last remaining community pubs in this part of London. Because of its special character it draws customers from all backgrounds from the surrounding streets – including elderly residents from Ashton Court old people's home who would find it impossible to walk to other pubs." The campaign has the support of Camra's Good Beer

Guide – it has won special mentions for its ales and atmosphere – and Time Out; they list the pub every year in their guide to London's best bars.

A Camra spokesman said the pub was vital to the area. "It is a classic pub which we do not want to see lost," he said.

Historian Gillian Tindall, who wrote a history of Kentish Town, backed the campaign, saying: "If Camden give permission for this change of use, they will be assisting the kind of social vandalism they are there to prevent."

The developers, Crossier Holdings Ltd., based in Holborn, declined to comment.

PINEAPPLE RESCUE

"THE CREAM OF LEVERTON STREET**"**

PINEAPPLE

WHERE NOTHING MAKES SENSE **ANY MORE**

THE PINEAPPLE, LEVERTON STREET, IS CLOSING
on the 19 December 2001.
Developers plan to change the pub into four flats.
In order to have any chance of the Pineapple surviving as a pub
we will need to make a combined and concerted attack on
Camden's Planning Department, **before 28 December 2001**.

Detailed information on ways in which you can help are available
in the corner shop (Mehmet's) and behind the Pineapple bar.

**" THE CREAM OF
LEVERTON STREET "**
PINEAPPLE
WHERE NOTHING MAKES SENSE
ANY MORE

THE PINEAPPLE IS CLOSING on the 19 December 2001.
The completion date for the sale of the Pineapple is 21 December 2001.
Developers have put in a planning application to change the pub into
four flats and to build a two storey office in the grounds in the mews.

In order to have any chance of the Pineapple surviving as a pub we will
have to, formally, lodge objections to the proposals. Camden counts every
letter or e-mail they receive. Your letter or e-mail is vital; if there are two (or more)
in a household, **each of you** should comment.
Comments have to be at the Camden office **before 28 December 2001.**

The letter/e-mail should be headed with the following details:
Application number: PEX0100941
Re: The Pineapple Public House, 51 Leverton Street
Proposal: Change of use of former pub building,
with roof extension, to provide 3x maisonettes & 1x flat.
New structure facing Railey Mews being a B1 office unit with parking space.

Comments
Your objections to the proposals might be:
• the loss of our traditional neighbourhood community pub as the focus of this residential area;
• loss of a public amenity;
• change of character in this environmental area;
• safety aspect – it is, unusually round here, a safe pub for women and the elderly on their own;
• proposed changes to outside of building.
Use your own words. Keep it brief and to the point.

Letters should be addressed to
Case officer John Davies
Development Control and Planning Services
London Borough of Camden
Town Hall
Argyle Street
London WC1H 8ND

e-mails env.devcon@camden.gov.uk
If sending an e-mail please include your full postal address.

Please tell all your friends who care about the Pineapple and get them to write to Camden.

If you want to see a copy of the application and the plans they are behind the counter at Mehmet's shop.
If you can offer any practical help or advice to the campaign please call Elisabeth Ingles 020 7485 5079
e-mail pineapple @scotthunter.co.uk   or leave a note at Mehmet's shop.

62 warriors launched campaign

A 'public meeting' was held on the evening of Wednesday 12 December in the pre-school/infant school room, at the Church of Our Lady Help of Christians, Lady Margaret Road. Amongst the sand pit, the toy store and the book corner, chairs of Lilliputian proportions were arranged to accommodate the interested, the weary and the arthritic. Local councillors, broadcasters, writers, three lawyers, planners and people who knew of 'potential buyers' came out of the woodwork with offers of 'help'. Two CAMRA officers fell into the meeting, in a state of shock, having first, inadvertently, slid into the Alcoholics Anonymous meeting in the adjacent room.

Drinkers fight to stop Pineapple being sliced up

By Sharon van Geuns

SINCE 1868 one of London's most treasured watering holes, The Pineapple in Leverton Street, Kentish Town, has sustained those living nearby.

But a battle is under way as regulars try to stop the Victorian public house being demolished and converted into flats and office space.

A campaign has been launched by the hundreds of people who use the pub, including actor Rufus Sewell, Ken Livingstone and Poet Laureate Andrew Motion. It is claimed by supporters that the pub's landlords agreed to sell after being "duped" by developers.

The Pineapple was put on the market by the widow and daughter of landlord Sean Gately when he died in October, on the understanding that the ground floor would remain a pub and the residential part above would be converted into flats.

The subsequent planning application lodged with Camden council by Crossier Properties Ltd involved turning the building into three maisonettes, a flat and a two-storey office at the back.

Campaigners are appealing to the council to deny Crossier permission and save the pub from meeting the same fate as at least a dozen others in the area.

Campaign leader Dr Jonty Boyce said: "There appears to be a terrible misunderstanding; the developers will be destroying a gem of a pub. It is the hub of community here. Many of The Pineapple's customers will simply have nowhere else to go."

Michael Balfour, another regular, said: "The Gately family have been duped. The pub is absolutely unique, with a classic interior full of original Victorian carvings, including pineapples."

Mr Sewell said: "The Pineapple is my favourite pub in London. It is the sort of pub me and my brother had to wait outside in the 1970s and be passed the occasional blackcurrant and lemonade and packet of crisps to keep us quiet.

"It still feels like a treat being allowed in. It would be a great shame if one of the last true community pubs in London had to go."

Mr Livingstone said: "It seems to me that The Pineapple is just the sort of local pub that is all too often disappearing. I think it should continue to serve the locals."

Actor Ken Stott, who is appearing in Faith Healer at the Almeida in King's Cross, said: "If it closes it means I will probably have to stop drinking. The Pineapple is a fantastic place where you can have a quiet pint without music blasting in your ear."

Last night Christine Gately, who with her mother Mary decided to sell the pub after her father died, said: "We are all really upset, this was never meant to happen. It's been hard enough losing my father, I feel terribly bad for the customers."

A hearing to decide the case will not take place until early January — although the pub is due to shut this Sunday.

A spokesman from Crossier said: "It's is still undecided what will happen although we understand a few people are unhappy. I am sorry to say that maybe the people who sold us the pub were a little naive. At the end of the day a good development offer was made and we took it."

A spokeswoman for Camden confirmed receipt of the application from Crossier and said it would be considered early in the New Year. The spokeswoman added: "We will of course consider the views of local people."

Public spirit: Pineapple regulars Ken Livingstone and Rufus Sewell want to save it from the developers

Campaigners Picture by Polly Hancock

LONDON Mayor Ken Livingstone has joined calls to stop a popular Kentish Town watering hole from closing down.

The Pineapple – affectionately known as the "luvvies" pub – was sold on October 20 to developers Crossier Properties Ltd on the understanding that the ground floor would continue to function as a pub.

But last week landlady Mary Gately, 66, who is leaving the pub following the recent death of husband Sean, discovered that a planning application to convert the entire building in Leverton Street into four flats and a two-storey office had been lodged with Camden Council.

Their daughter Christine said: "I was absolutely stunned. It is not what we wanted at all. My mum is worried the regulars will think we have sold them down the river.

"We have turned down hundreds of buyers because they wanted to shut the pub down and we sold it for half the amount we wanted on the understanding it would remain a pub."

Regulars have mounted a vigorous campaign to fight the proposals and formed a committee to lobby local councillors and the London Mayor for support.

They are also taking legal advice over whether they can keep the pub open when the Gatelys leave on Sunday.

In a statement issued by Mr Livingstone, he said: "Local facilities – including places to relax and socialise – are vital to provide a sense of community. It seems to me that The Pineapple is the sort of local pub that is all too often disappearing in London. I think it should continue to serve the local community."

Originally a brothel, The Pineapple was built in 1868. It is also known as the "luvvies" pub because of the actors and artists who frequent it. Rufus Sewell, star of the film A Knight's Tale who lives in nearby Leighton Place, former Dr Who and Hampstead resident Sylvester McCoy and The Vice star Ken Stott are all regulars.

Mr Stott is said to have based his current part starring in the Almeida's production of Brian Friel's play Faith Healer on the late landlord.

Campaign organiser Elisabeth Ingles, 58, of Ascham Street, Kentish Town, who has been a regular at the Pineapple for 25 years, said: "It has a distinctive

Stage set for keep 'luvvies

Last orders are being called at The Pineapple in Rufus Sewell and Sylvester McCoy. **Stephen L**

Campaigners (from left) Gill Scott, Michael Balfour, Elisabeth Ingl

social character. People in The Pineapple look out for each other.

"Unlike some local pubs, it has no 'rough trade' and has not had to call out the police in recent memory. Hardly any other pub in the area has this particular atmosphere and women on their own feel perfectly safe."

Ham&High cartoonist Ken Pyne, 50, of Southcote Road, Tufnell Park, is a Pineapple regular. He said: "It will be a tremendous loss to the community if it closes and a loss to Camden. It is mentioned in all the guide books."

Pineapple regular Jon Rake added: "There are surely some

or a battl
s' pub open

in Kentish Town – a favourite of stars such as

Lucas reports on the campaign to save it

es and Alison Watt.

Picture by Polly Hancock

things more important than making a quick buck. I believe Camden is a socialist authority."

Camden is due to consider the application in January after a period of consultation with residents this month.

A council spokesman said: "We are listening to any objections residents have to the devel-opment and if they think the pub is an integral part of their community we will certainly take that into account when considering the application."

Crossier Properties Ltd declined to comment on the proposals.

editorial@hamhigh.co.uk

"RESCUE T-SHIRTS"

HAVE ALL BEEN SOLD
BUT
WE WILL PRINT MORE
IF THERE IS A DEMAND

PLEASE LEAVE YOUR NAME, ADDRESS AND PHONE NUMBER
WITH MEHMET. WHEN WE HAVE A LARGE ENOUGH ORDER (24)
WE WILL CONTACT YOU, TELL YOU HOW MUCH (£10–£12) &
WHEN THEY WILL BE READY.

Don't forget to give us your size
adults BLACK SHORT SLEEVE: XL   L   M
adults BLACK LONG SLEEVE: XL   L   M

children BLACK SHORT SLEEVE: L   M   S
children RED LONG SLEEVE WITH HOOD: L   M   S

Funds were needed to run the campaign. T-shirts [nearly 200], sold for a minimum contribution of £5, raised £1,399.00. The Gatelys had to leave the pub empty on 21 December; Mary and Christine offered for sale the memorabilia, collected over the previous fourteen years, which covered the shelves of the back-bar and the walls of the darts room. With people offering silly amounts of money for memories [newspaper cuttings, drawings, prints, the darts board, the bell] the sale raised £1,056.80. At the end of the evening the Pineapple closed.

remained closed 155 days

SPECIAL AUCTION

OF

PINEAPPLE MEMORABILIA

MOSTLY DONATED BY CHRISTINE AND MARY

WEDNESDAY

19

DECEMBER

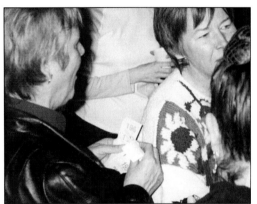

The pub was spot-listed in eight days.
In 2001 there were 8007 listed pubs in
England. There were about 400 in all the
London boroughs, 54 in Camden; most are
very grand, the Pineapple is comparatively
humble.

What difference did the listing make?
It stopped the developer in his tracks;
he could not develop the building.
His architects were invited by Camden to
withdraw their plans. The publicity about
the listing lost the developer his finance;
it made 'locals' aware that the pub could
be 'inadvertently' demolished – providing
a natural security ring around the building.

The whole building, its fabric inside and
out, and the pub fittings and fixtures are
listed. It is unlikely that permission will
ever be given for anything other than a pub
to operate on the premises.

Pineapple listed in 8 days

Department for Culture, Media and Sport
Architecture and Historic Environment Division

2-4 Cockspur Street
London SW1Y 5DH
www.culture.gov.uk

Tel 020 7211 6910
Fax 020 7211 6962
saima.mirza
@culture.gsi.gov.uk

Gill Scott and Associates
48 Rochester Place
London
NW1 9JX

Your Ref:

Our Ref: SL-1454-01

18 December 2001

Dear Ms Scott

PLANNING (LISTED BUILDINGS AND CONSERVATION AREAS) ACT 1990
BUILDINGS OF SPECIAL ARCHITECTURAL OR HISTORIC INTEREST
PINEAPPLE PUBLIC HOUSE, NO. 51 LEVERTON STREET, LONDON, NW5

I refer to your letter asking the Secretary of State to consider the above building for inclusion in the Statutory List.

After careful consideration of all the evidence, including advice from English Heritage, the Secretary of State has decided to list the building. It was added to the list on 18th December 2001 in Grade II having been judged to be a building of special architectural or historic interest. I enclose a copy of the list entry for your information.

Yours sincerely

Saima Mirza
Listing and Archaeology Branch

INVESTOR IN PEOPLE

SCHEDULE

The following building shall be added to the list:-

LEVERTON STREET
No. 51
789-1/0/10190   **Pineapple Public House**

II

The Pineapple public house. C.1868. Builder unknown. Yellow stock brick. Stucco-faced ground floor, moulded stone window arches. Double valley roof not visible behind parapet. EXTERIOR: three-bay elevation, three storeys high, with doorway to centre flanked by windows with three-panel aprons; all openings are segmental-headed, with pineapple motifs to keystones. Upper windows are 2/2-pane sashes. Ground floor is faced with channelled rustication, with moulded imposts, radiating voussoirs, and a modillion cornice at first floor level, carried on acanthus-enriched brackets at each end. Curved corner to south-east with raised quoins of brick. Side elevation to south continues ground floor rustication, with subsidiary door (now blocked)and window; three windows to first floor (western pair blind), one to second floor. INTERIOR: altered, but retains good behind-bar screen with etched glass mirrors depicting vases of flowers with pineapples below; frieze contains mirrored lettering reading WHISKIES BRANDIES WINES; frieze is carried on four Corinthian pilasters with mirrored strips decorated with lotus leafs; rear counter is carried on consoles with pineapple decoration. Ceiling to main bar retains decorative plaster cornice. An unusually exuberant example of a mid-Victorian pub serving a newly-built development of suburban housing, which, in spite of internal alteration, retains a fine behind-bar screen.

Signed by authority of the
Secretary of State

KENNEDY HUMPHREYS
Department for Culture, Media and Sport

Dated: 18 DECEMBER 2007

1

Protestors' jo
status win fo

RENEGADE Kentish Town campaigners have scuppered plans to shut down their local watering hole.

Regulars at the Pineapple Pub in Leverton Street, Kentish Town were distraught at plans to close the community boozer and turn it into flats.

With the backing of stars from stage and screen, the well-connected campaigners launched a media campaign to stop the plans.

And on Tuesday they scored their first major victory against developers Crossier Properties Ltd, when the Pineapple was granted emergency listed status by English Heritage.

Delighted campaign leader Doctor Jonty Boyce said: "As of now the Pineapple is a Grade-II listed building.

"That means the developers are not allowed to make any changes to

By **CAROLINE RYDER**

the exterior or specified parts of the interior.

"If they do, it's a criminal offence and they could go to jail.

"It's great news, but we're not going to get complacent – we will be setting up surveillance patrols over Christmas to make sure nothing about the pub is changed."

Despite the eleventh hour reprieve, the Pineapple is still in the hands of Crossier Ltd, who bought the building in October.

So regulars still had to endure the closure of their beloved pub on Wednesday, when the keys were handed over to Crossier as originally planned. Dr Boyce said:"At the moment we can only speculate on the future.

"No doubt Crossier will want to

94

oy at special
r closing pub

find a buyer to get the pub off their hands now they can't turn it into soulless flats.

"We can only hope the new buyer will also want to keep the spirit of the Pineapple Pub alive."

■ LEFT to right: Michael Garne, Poison in drama London's Burning, actor Ken Stott, newsman Jon Snow and Roger Lloyd Pack, Trigger in Only Fools and Horses, join the protest to save The Pineapple pub last Staurday.
Picture: Tony Gay

Pineapple gets a celebrity boost – see page 3

Camden New Journal

Free Newspaper of the Year

Thursday December 20, 2001   An Independent Paper   No 1020

VFD VERIFIED FREE DISTRIBUTION BULK DISTRIBUTION

A merry Christmas to all our readers

The next New Journal will be published on Dec 27

4 January 2001 – 28 June 2001
Average Bulk Distribution 61,364

MP's televised attack on religious schools angers Bishop of Edmonton

Celebrities

Pine boos

by DAN CARRIER

THE battle to save a Kentish Town pub has been boosted by a Government decision to list the building.

Campaigners, including Channel Four news anchorman Jon Snow and actors Rufus Sewell and Roger Lloyd-Pack, have been fighting to stop their local, the Pineapple, being turned in to yuppie flats. They were told earlier this week the building had been given Grade II listed status which could radically alter developers' plans for the site.

English Heritage recommended the listing, which stops changes to the facade and the bar area, to the Department of Culture, Media and Sport after regulars told them of the pub's plight.

The Pineapple, in Leverton Street, was sold to a development company after publican Sean Gately died in November.

The Gately family, who have run the pub since 1987, sold the site for £500,000 – well below its market value – on the understanding it would remain open, with developers renovating flats upstairs.

Days after the deal had been signed and the verbal agreement made, new owners Crossier Properties Ltd put in an application to turn the pub into luxury maisonettes and a back yard area into a two-storey office.

es rally to save their local pub from closure

eapple's plight sted by listing

Pineapple mates: (from left) Michael Garner from London's Burning, actors Ken Stott and Roger Lloyd-Pack, and Jon Snow, outside the Pineapple pub. Inset, Rufus Sewell

Jonty Boyce, a regular who is heading the campaign, told the New Journal that he hoped the listing would make it harder for the developers. He said: "We applied last week and are thrilled the department granted listed status. The fight is not over yet, but it is one more hurdle the developers will have to overcome."

Council planning chief Councillor Brian Woodrow told the New Journal that developers would have to take the listed status in to account when they made their application.

The battle to save the pub – which has led to Camden Council being sent hundreds of letters and e-mails asking them to turn down the application – has been supported by a host of celebrities who drink there.

Actor Rufus Sewell, who lives in nearby Leighton Road, said the pub was an essential part of the neighbourhood.

He said: "It is the sort of place I used to wait outside while my parents had a drink in the 1970s. It is a local asset and we should be protecting the places that make our community special."

Channel Four anchorman Jon Snow, who lives opposite, also leant his weight to the campaign. He said: "We do not need these houses. It will be bring more traffic and they are designed with posh people – like myself – in mind."

Roger Lloyd-Pack – Trigger from Only Fools and Horses – has popped in for a beer many times over the years while living in neighbouring Lady Margaret road.

He said he would be devastated if the plans went ahead. He said: "It is a proper pub. It is a vital cog in keeping the community together. If it goes, the community will become more and more fractured."

Development company Crossier Properties are refusing to discuss their plans.

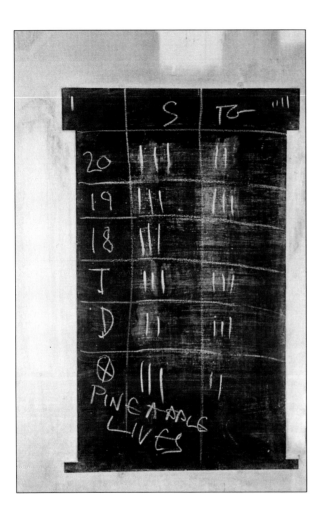

Stephen Lucas

CAMPAIGNERS have won a major victory in their battle to save The Pineapple pub, with news that it has been listed by English Heritage.

The Grade-II listing, announced on Tuesday, protects period Victorian features inside and outside the pub in Leverton Street, Kentish Town, and makes it highly unlikely that owners Crossier Properties Ltd will gain planning permission to convert it into flats and office space.

The Ham&High has learned that the firm, which bought the pub two months ago from landlady Mary Gately for around £500,000, is considering putting it back on the market.

When Crossier properties applied to turn it into four flats and a two-storey office, loyal regulars formed a committee to fight the proposals and applied to have the pub listed.

Clifford Green, a negotiator at Paramount Investments 2000, the company which acquired the Pineapple on behalf of Crossier Properties, described the issue as a "hot potato".

"The pub is not officially back on the market, but we have been approached by a lot of people, including publicans, who are interested in buying it," he said.

"If the price is right – around £700,000 – we will sell it. We are pursuing the planning application but at the same time we are keeping all of our options open."

The pub is affectionately called the "luvvies'" pub because of the actors who frequent it, and on Sunday they turned out in force to support the campaign.

English Heritage 'saves' Pineapple

Michael Garner, Ken Stott, Jon Snow and Roger Lloyd Pack pledge their support to the 'Pineapple' campaign.
Picture by Nigel Sutton

Only Fools and Horses star Roger Lloyd Pack, a regular at the pub for 12 years, said: "Shame on Camden if they accept this planning application.

"All those glossy brochures they produce about the value of the community will not be worth the paper they are written on."

Michael Garner, who stars in ITV drama London's Burning, travels from his home in Tufnell Park to reach The Pineapple.

"It's clear to a blind man this pub should stay," he said. "This pub is not about the actors who drink here, it has a long history of serving the local area. If we do not hang on to places like this we will have a very dull community."

Channel 4 newsreader Jon Snow, who lives in Kentish Town, said the plans were indefensible.

"The pub is not going to be turned into affordable housing," he said. "It is going to be for posh people with big cars, and there are enough posh people with big cars round here as it is."

Conservative councillor Stephen Hocking has urged Camden's planning committee to reject the planning application.

"If there is any point at all in local democracy, surely it is to listen to the wishes of the local residents. I hope the committee will see the harm that this application would cause and will reject it."

Camden is due to rule on the planning application early in the new year.

editorial@hamhigh.co.uk

Regulars

The Pineapple in Kentish Town

By Tony Bassett
and Mira Bar-Hillel

A GROUP of actors and newscasters, including Jon Snow and Roger Lloyd Pack, are celebrating the spot-listing of their favourite local pub.

The pub's regular users, including actors Ken Stott and Michael Garner from London's Burning, now expect the listing will prevent the famous Pineapple Pub in Kentish Town from being closed down and converted into flats and offices.

The Pineapple opened in 1868 and still has many of its original 19th century fittings, including the decorative glass area behind the

s win bar fight

Drinkers get pub listed in bid to stop developers

bar. When they learned that proposals to close the pub were being considered by developer Crossier Properties, local campaigners lobbied English Heritage to spot-list the historic Victorian pub.

A planning application was made to Camden council in November, and the campaign went into high gear — culminating in the listing last week. The listing means that the developers will have to get a special "listed building consent" for any major works. Buildings recently listed rarely get this consent. The planning system also encourages listed buildings to remain in their original use.

Campaign leader Dr Jonty Boyce said: "The Pineapple is now a Grade-II listed building and the developers are not allowed to make any changes to the exterior or specified parts of the interior without permission. If they do, it's a criminal offence and they could go to jail. It's great news but we are not going to get complacent."

Dr Boyce said the pub was currently closed, adding: "We will be setting up surveillance patrols over Christmas to make sure nothing about the pub is changed."

Another campaigner, Gill Scott, said: "A number of celebrities regularly come to the pub for a quiet drink and were happy to support our campaign to keep it open.

Ms Scott added: "Prince Charles recently spoke about how important the village pub was as a centre of life in a rural community. This is just like a village pub, only it is in London."

Charles cheers Ken with his pub stance

Ken Stott, pictured in his role in the Faith Healer at the Almeida.

KENTISH Town actor Ken Stott appears to agree with Prince Charles' views on turning local pubs into the "hub" of the community.

This week Prince Charles teamed up with the Countryside Agency to produce a guide entitled Make the Pub the Hub, which urges publicans to transform rural pubs into one-stop shops, selling videos, groceries and even hangover remedies.

The very much city-based Mr Stott, who played Detective Inspector Pat Chappel in ITV drama series The Vice, echoed the Prince when he spoke to Heathman on Sunday at an event to save his local pub, The Pineapple, in Leverton Street, Kentish Town.

"I am always keen that pubs should change the way they operate, and this can be done in many good ways," he said.

"Entertainment can be added, art galleries could be included, or food can be served.

"To close a small pub down completely is to destroy the community."

Landlord was always one of the inn crowd

MR Stott based parts of the character he plays in Faith Healer at the Almeida Theatre on Sean Gately, the landlord of the Pineapple who died in October.

"Sean was a generous hearted, soft and charming man," he said. "There is a lot of him living in the character I play, like his charm, and sometimes I hear his voice in the character."

Film star Rufus Sewell, who lives in Leighton Place, Kentish Town, has also been among those backing the campaign to save the historic pub.

"You get an incredible mix in here," said the brooding heartthrob, who starred in A Knight's Tale and Middlemarch.

"It is unusual in a world where we have pubs for gay people, pubs for straight people, ones for black people, and others for white people.

"The Pineapple is not homogenised or McDonaldsised. It is everything an English pub should be."

Non-actors go to the Pineapple too

YOUR story about the threatened Pineapple in Kentish Town (Ham&High, December 14) may have given the misleading impression that it is a "luvvies' pub".

Because one or two struggling actors and media personalities have jumped on the bandwagon in order to get their pictures in the paper, it does not follow that they are in any way representative!

That is, of course, a joke – all the regulars and local people involved in the fight to prevent the closure for redevelopment of this excellent venue are grateful for the amazing support received from so many quarters.

The Pineapple is not merely a watering hole for well-heeled actors and their ilk, but a truly cosmopolitan, community-based social amenity, one great feature of which is the irrelevance of anybody's occupation and class – not to mention race, sexual orientation, age, gender, financial status and dress sense.

Equality rather than Equity gets top billing at the Pineapple.

MARTIN JAMES
Leverton Street, NW5 2NX

534 wrote to the council. The planners at Camden council had not previously, nor since, received such a large number of written responses to a planning application [less than 20 is most usual, more than 40 is the exception]. 533 responses were objections; one man emailed twice to ask for the name and address of the developer to express his interest in buying one of the flats.

533
supporters wrote to council

George Orwell wrote in the *Evening Standard* in 1946 about the qualities of his perfect pub [see next page] ...*If you are asked why you favour a particular public-house, it would seem natural to put the beer first, but the thing that most appeals to me about the* Moon Under Water *is what people call its 'atmosphere'.*

55 years later 533 people would have been happy to tell him to check out their pub which fitted most of his criteria. 533 supporters wrote passionately [some in two lines, some over two pages] to describe what the Pineapple pub meant to them personally; all wrote about 'atmosphere', a few talked about the beer. 90% wrote from addresses within half a mile of the pub; some from the edges of Camden, London, Ireland, Canada, Australia and Europe. A large number declared their age – the youngest was ten, the oldest in their 80s – and how long they had been 'going' to the Pineapple; more than 65% were women. Every letter contained one or more of these words **special, friendly, welcoming, unique, rare, community, social focus, neighbourhood, heart of community, all ages, all walks of life, safe, safe for women [on their own], without threat of nuisance [violence, abuse].** About half of the responses started with "I am very upset... "I am horrified... "I am most distressed... "When I heard it was about to close I just couldn't believe it..."; parting shots included "...please stop it". "...please don't let this happen". "...I hope you will consider our feelings". "...I do hope the Council will not let us down". "BE BOLD & BE BRAVE & SAY NO". "...Come on, stop it now". "GO ON – show local people you are listening". "...my faith in local democracy will be severely under-mined if planning permission for this proposal is granted". "It would be no less than a tragedy and a disgrace if Camden approve this application and if they do so, I personally will never vote Labour again" [sent from Co Donegal]. "...I invite you to sample the **atmosphere** for yourself and I assure you if you do you will be writing one of these emails yourself". The really polite thanked the planners for reading their letters and wished them a Happy Christmas.

London Evening Standard
9 February 1946

George Orwell in his Saturday essay tells the secrets of his favourite public-house The Moon Under Water

MY favourite public-house, the *Moon Under Water*, is only two minutes from a bus stop, but it is on a side-street, and drunks and rowdies never seem to find their way there, even on Saturday nights.

Its clientele, though fairly large, consists mostly of "regulars" who occupy the same chair every evening and go there for conversation as much as for the beer.

If you are asked why you favour a particular public-house, it would seem natural to put the beer first, but the thing that most appeals to me about the *Moon Under Water* is what people call its "atmosphere."

To begin with, its whole architecture and fittings are uncompromisingly Victorian. It has no glass-topped tables or other modern miseries, and, on the other hand, no sham roof-beams, ingle-nooks or plastic panels masquerading as oak. The grained woodwork, the ornamental mirrors behind the bar, the cast-iron fireplaces, the florid ceiling stained dark yellow by tobacco-smoke, the stuffed bull's head over the mantelpiece — everything has the solid, comfortable ugliness of the nineteenth century.

Quiet enough to talk

In winter there is generally a good fire burning in at least two of the bars, and the Victorian lay-out of the place gives one plenty of elbow-room. There are a public bar, a saloon bar, a ladies' bar, a bottle-and-jug for those who are too bashful to buy their supper beer publicly, and, upstairs, a dining-room.

Games are only played in the public, so that in the other bars you can walk about without constantly ducking to avoid flying darts.

In the *Moon Under Water* it is always quiet enough to talk. The house possesses neither a radio nor a piano, and even on Christmas Eve and such occasions the singing that happens is of a decorous kind.

The barmaids know most of their customers by name, and take a personal interest in everyone. They are all middle-aged women —

two of them have their hair dyed in quite surprising shades — and they call everyone 'dear', irrespective of age or sex ('Dear', not 'Ducky: pubs where the barmaid calls you 'ducky' always have a disagreeable raffish atmosphere).

A good, solid lunch

Unlike most pubs, the *Moon Under Water* sells tobacco as well as cigarettes, and it also sells aspirins and stamps, and is obliging about letting you use the telephone.

You cannot get dinner at the *Moon Under Water*, but there is always the snack counter where you can get liver-sausage sandwiches, mussels (a speciality of the house), cheese, pickles and those large biscuits with caraway seeds in them which only seem to exist in public-houses.

Upstairs, six days a week, you can get a good, solid lunch — for example, a cut off the joint, two vegetables and boiled jam roll — for about three shillings.

The special pleasure of this lunch is that you can have draught stout with it. I doubt whether as many as 10 per cent of London pubs serve draught stout, but the *Moon Under Water* is one of them. It is a soft, creamy sort of stout, and it goes better in a pewter pot.

They are particular about their drinking vessels at the *Moon Under Water*, and never, for example, make the mistake of serving a pint of beer in a handleless glass. Apart from glass and pewter mugs, they have some of those pleasant strawberry-pink china ones which are now seldom seen in London. China mugs went out about 30 years ago, because most people like their drink to be transparent, but in my opinion beer tastes better out of china.

The garden is a surprise

The great surprise of the *Moon Under Water* is its garden. You go through a narrow passage leading out of the saloon, and find yourself in a fairly large garden with plane trees, under which there are little green tables with iron chairs round them. Up at one end of the garden there are swings and a chute for the children.

On summer evenings there are family parties, and you sit under the plane trees having beer or draught cider to the tune of delighted squeals from children going down the chute. The prams with the younger children are parked near the gate.

Many as are the virtues of the *Moon Under Water*, I think that the garden is its best feature, because it allows whole families to go there instead of Mum having to stay at home and mind the baby while Dad goes out alone.

And though, strictly speaking, they are only allowed in the garden, the children tend to seep into the pub and even to fetch drinks for their parents. This, I believe, is against the law, but it is a law that deserves to be broken, for it is the puritanical nonsense of excluding children — and therefore, to some extent, women — from pubs that has turned these places into mere boozing-shops instead of the family gathering-places that they ought to be.

Do you know of one

The *Moon Under Water* is my ideal of what a pub should be — at any rate, in the London area. (The qualities one expects of a country pub are slightly different.)

But now is the time to reveal something which the discerning and disillusioned reader will probably have guessed already. There is no such place as the *Moon Under Water*.

That is to say, there may well be a pub of that name, but I don't know of it, nor do I know any pub with just that combination of qualities.

I know pubs where the beer is good but you can't get meals, others where you can get meals but which are noisy and crowded, and others which are quiet but where the beer is generally sour. As for gardens, offhand I can only think of three London pubs that possess them.

⌨

But, to be fair, I do know of a few pubs that almost come up to the *Moon Under Water*. I have mentioned above ten qualities that the perfect pub should have and I know one pub that has eight of them. Even there, however, there is no draught stout, and no china mugs.

And if anyone knows of a pub that has draught stout, open fires, cheap meals, a garden, motherly barmaids and no radio, I should be glad to hear of it, even though its name were something as prosaic as the *Red Lion* or the *Railway Arms*.

Eric Blair lived in Parliament Hill and in Kentish Town (Lawford Road) 1935-1936.

For the first time in 133 years customers, regulars, neighbours and friends had the unusual task of finding the words to describe the Pineapple and to send them to 'strangers' at the Council. Extracts cover the depth of feelings – all points made were not necessarily planning issues.

"I have one point to make resisting the ambitions of would-be developers of the Pineapple. The Pineapple is not simply a show-case for celebrities, though given the area, it is a reflection. I have lived here for seven years, met and been welcomed by a wide range of locals from priest to plumber and through all between and around. This place is safe, secure and gives substance to that often arid word: community".

"...I will no longer have a lounge away from home in which I can entertain many of my foreign friends who all cherish the Pineapple for its uniqueness throughout London, if not the world".

"The Pineapple is a true community pub. There is a very warm atmosphere, and as a colleague once said 'it is like being invited into a friend's back room for a drink'".

"I am an infrequent but devoted customer of the Pineapple. As a visitor to Britain, the Pineapple presents a side of your country that is sadly missing elsewhere – a gathering place for a community. To suggest that another pub might replace the Pineapple would be to miss what community is".

"It is a safe pub where both my wife and I have waited while we have been locked out (which we do because we have been disorganised)".

"We leave our spare keys at the pub..."

"...we went to the pub for help getting into our house".

"I have relied on the Pineapple when I have been locked out of my flat, needed to find out about local plumbers, electricians..."

"The closure of the Pineapple has torn the heart from my Christmas, and has deprived me of celebrating the festival with the rest of my community which I consider to be a basic right for a citizen of London".

'...and another reason I proposed to my wife in the Pineapple...'

"The Pineapple was my local for the best part of thirty years…"
"I grew up and lived in the area for forty years and the Pineapple featured seriously in my own personal history as a pub I cut my teeth in, met my partner in and still have many friends in…"

"Living so close as I do to the Pub I have to live with its 'bad side' eg late night noise etc, but I would not have it any other way because of its importance to our community".

"Although I am not a regular pub user, I consider that a well run local pub can be an asset to neighbourhood communities".

"I myself am not a great pub-goer and rarely went there; but the Pineapple is a special place, a safe place for any members of the community to go…"

"This letter might sound strange coming as it does, from a past director of Alcohol Concern and [a past] chair of CASA (though I stress I'm writing in a personal capacity) …Those of us who favour sensible drinking, rather than alcohol abuse, know that smaller, friendly drinking venues, with a familiar clientele, popular with locals and welcoming to older people, is a much safer environment [than the anonymous, pressure-to-drink environments offered by many other venues in Camden]. The Pineapple is a place messages can be left, contacts made, and people 'watched out' for. The pub, and the invaluable shop opposite, give this part of Kentish Town its character and popularity and prevent it being just another large housing area".

"Kentish Town hasn't got much going for it.
            Please don't rob it of the best it has to offer".

"The Pineapple represents, in short, a last bastion of village London and as such should be given a preservation order, not a death warrant".

"Far from being a former pub, the Pineapple is a vibrant, popular local pub, serving as the hub of a genuine community, and should be maintained as such at all costs. The Pineapple serves as a meeting place, a local forum, and a source of community news and activity. It is here that we find out who is ill, or short of cash, or looking for a job, or accidentally locked out of the house, or in any way in need of assistance. The pub provides the conduit for the kind of positive social behaviour now rarely seen in the urban environment, and without which social cohesion disappears, and the neighbourhood becomes a problem, both for residents and for the local authorities".

Dear Mr Davies

It is with shock and upset I am writing to you, after finding out yesterday evening, that my local public house, the Pineapple, is about to be closed for re-development.

I moved to the area about three years ago, and found myself living on Lady Margaret Road. It was at this time that I 'discovered' the Pineapple and met so many of the people who have become firm friends and allies in a city renowned for alienation – in a world where people are becoming more and more lonely, the pub has proved to be a refreshing and important contrast to this stereotype. When we had to move out, my primary criterion, when speaking to estate agents, was "IT MUST BE IN WALKING DISTANCE OF THE PINEAPPLE" – I kid you not!

When September 11 occurred, after work was cut short early, I returned home and immediately left for the pub. Why? I wanted to be with people – in a communal area with the mutual respect and friendship that can only really ever develop in a local public house.

Public houses have an important part to play in the community – they remove one from the family situations/tensions, they provide a platform for the local communities to relate and feel a part of a greater whole and they are unique in the manner in which people come together. Most locals only see each other in the pub, and there is protocol adhered to, not found elsewhere, which makes it a special place to be.

If Camden Council chooses to go along with these developers, they will have let down the community that they are there to serve – they will have supported the commercialisation and destruction of the local amenities we all hold dear. And the end result of this? Yet another property developer gets rich while the locals suffer. I do not believe Camden Council would want to propagate such negative culture, and I implore you to ensure this abuse of a local focal point does not go ahead. *SW [objection number 511]*

DEAR John Davies Please don't close the Pineapple Pub, if you need a reason not to just visit and have a drink and you will see how great it is. *WB [obj330]*

Hello there – Please don't close the Pineapple! It has saved my life this winter when my central heating broke down and I couldn't afford to fix it – as a single woman there isn't another similar pub in the area that I would have felt comfortable to sit in for a night. If you would like to ask me any further questions my address is... *NB [obj312]*

Dear Mr Davies ...I have lived in all parts of London for twenty years, and never known a pub like it – and it was one of the main reasons I moved here two and a half years ago. The day I looked at my house before buying it I popped into the Pineapple for a drink and bumped into a friend who lived in the neighbourhood, who was there with one of his neighbours. The next day I popped in again and met a different friend, who was there with another neighbour, and I fell so much in love with the friendly close-knit community that revolves around the Pineapple that I had to live nearby...". *AB [obj156]*.

Dear Sir/Madam

"... my concerns as to the proposed change of use focus on the loss of a vital community asset. The area of North Kentish Town is one where a number of pubs have recently closed, and where there are few if any truly local meeting points which are not regularly overwhelmed by visitors to the area. [...] Having got to know the area, the community feeling around Ascham Street was a major reason why I chose to move here. Children are able to play football in the roadway, all the neighbours know one another, and there is overall a sense of belonging, which is very rare in London today. One of the key focal points of this community spirit (together with its adjacent corner shop) is the Pineapple. Its location, and reputation, have made it an alternative "front room" for a great part of the local area. It is one of those very rare London pubs which is just as full at 6.00pm on a Tuesday as 9.00pm on a Saturday, for the very reason that it is part of the community, rather than a destination for those from other communities. It also attracts customers from all parts of this community – a pink-haired punk is quite likely to be found sitting at the bar next to two elderly ladies from Ascham Court home, who will presumably now have no alternative recreational destination whatsoever within walking distance. It is also a destination – sadly unusual around Kentish Town – which single women are happy to visit alone. A high proportion of the houses along Leverton and Ascham Streets are now displaying 'Pineapple Rescue' posters. The views of the local community are clear. I very much look forward to hearing that Camden Council has fulfilled the clear mandate of this local community by rejecting this planning application, and encouraging the developers to accept one of the several alternative offers available..." *NT [obj67]*.

Dear John "I have never written to the council to oppose planning applications before but then I have never felt so strongly about building changes as I do about the proposed change of use for the Pineapple [...]" *[obj288]*

Dear John Davis I write to object to the closure of the above public house. The Pineapple is a rare place where people of many kinds meet and drink in an atmosphere of tolerance. Last Saturday for example I had a good conversation with a house painter and a barrister (the former spoke rather more sense I thought!). It is a genuine local which 'polices' itself and a real community resource – the helping and social networks there have evolved over years and have not been 'prescribed' by some distant autocratic authority as an unwholesome patriarchal/matriarchal blend of 'do-good-ery'. It is the best Advice Centre I know and so much cheaper than therapy!

At the recent Memorial Mass for the late landlord Mr Gately, Father Stewart of the Church of Our Lady Help of Christians drew telling parallels between the roles of publican and priest. Certainly the real but non-sectarian fellowship of 'The Pineapple' has helped keep me on the rails over the last 25 years! [...] *JR [obj190]*

Dear Sir or Madam

Please please don't take our local pub away from us. So many old people rely on the Pineapple to go and have a quiet drink & to sit there & to know it's safe & we are all one big happy Family.

Old people go regularly for a drink & a chat, some only live over the road some a few doors away; that keeps them going, any further they couldn't manage it & by not staying as the pub we all love, everyone would feel the loss.

I've lived in Leverton Street for 25 years. I suffer with heart trouble, kidney trouble & knowing all the people who go in the Pineapple there's always someone with a wave & smile at you & ask if you're alright. I am an Elderly Lady in my late 70s; my husband who was in poor health used to manage to get over for his pint. The young people arrange to meet there & plan an evening out.

I ask you to see if anything can be done to keep our spirits going & leave our pub as it is. Yours sincerely *Mrs I H [obj169]*.

Dear Mr Davies

Save the Pineapple

I was dismayed to hear of the proposed closure of this pub and its conversion into flats. It might be thought that this is nothing to do with someone living in Gloucestershire, but it seems to me that this is a matter of much more than local concern. I have been an enthusiast for the traditional British pub ever since I was old enough to drink in one – and, to be honest, a little before that as well – and I have written on the subject in my travel books and in my history of beer and pubs, *Opening Time.*

I know The Pineapple well, and it seems to me to have unique qualities which cannot easily be replaced. Architecturally, it is a typical small Victorian town pub, and in particular the back bar retains many of its original features. But if this were all it had to offer, then I would be saddened by its closure, but would probably not be moved to do very much about it. What seems to me to be much more important is that this is a survivor of a diminishing band of real pubs, serving a local community. It is a place to meet and talk, without having to shout over a never-ending torrent of over-amplified music. It is a place where people come to enjoy a drink, without being made to feel that they are intruding, occupying space that could be used more profitably for serving food. It follows no trends, does not try and find themes, but simply offers good beer in traditional surroundings that have mellowed comfortably through a century and a half of use. It is a pub which does what the best pubs have always done – welcomes everyone, young or old, male or female. It is not the only pub in the area, so that the situation might be thought not quite comparable to that of a village pub under threat. But this is the equivalent of the village pub. This is the one where all sections of the community really do feel comfortably at home, and its place can never be taken by a large high street establishment.

If the Pineapple is converted into flats, something of immense value will be lost to the community. I am only an occasional visitor, though a visit to friends in the area rarely goes by without calling in at some time during the stay. But even the occasional visitor is soon aware that this is something special, a pub to relax in, a pub where drink is what it should be – a lubricant to conversation, not an end in itself. There are Victorian pubs in London which have more spectacular features, grander engraved glass, older fixtures, but they do not necessarily have the sense of intimacy that comes with this modest, friendly, welcoming establishment. It is, quite literally, irreplaceable.

Anthony Burton
Author, broadcaster
Stroud, Gloucestershire
10 December 2001

Re PEX 0100941 ◯BJ   92

PINEAPPLE
  51 LEVERTON St
     NW5

Hester Boyce.
20 Raudey St.
Kentish town.
London.
NW5 2HU.

Dear MR Davis,

If you close down the Pineapple pub It would not only be unfair but it would disrupt the local comunity. Where would everyone go? What would everyone do? The answer is nothing, there are no others pups like the pineapple near us! When I was about six or seven I went there with my dad to play dominoes and learnt my three and five times tables.

I feel that it is discraesfull to do such a thing to this sort of happy, jolly, and freindly atmos-pheric meeting place. PLEASE HELP US!!!

        Loue
          from
          Hester Boyle
                            aged 10 years!

        HESTER   BOYCE.

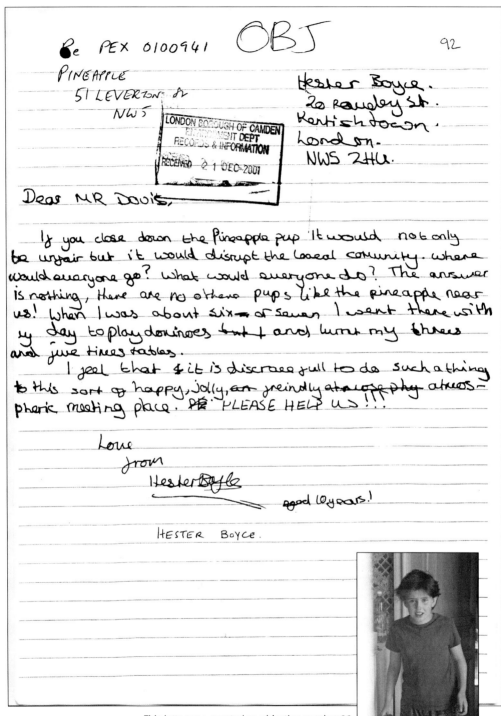

This letter was counted as *objection number 92*

428

The Old Brewery, Tadcaster. Established 1758

FOR MILD AND BITTER
BEERS AND STOUT

SAMUEL SMITH
(SOUTHERN)

Fax No:
TADCASTER (01937) 834673

Telephone No:
TADCASTER (01937) 832225

Reg. No. 1345661 England

YOUR REF

OUR REF   Prop/mrb

The Old Brewery,
TADCASTER
NORTH YORKSHIRE LS24 9SB

J. Davies Esq.
Development Control Team
Environment Department
Camden Council
6th Floor, Camden Town Hall Extension
Argyle Street
LONDON WC1H 8EQ

14th December 2001

Dear Mr Davies,

Case File F12/2/9. Planning Application PEX0100941 – The Pineapple public house

Further to our telephone conversation earlier today regarding the above planning application, I am writing to express our company's interest in purchasing The Pineapple public house.

Having visited the site on 13th December 2001 I can confirm that contrary to the details given in sections 2, 3 and 8 of the application, the pub has not yet closed and it would be our intention to retain the premises for trading as a traditional public house if, of course, a sale could be agreed at some stage in the future. However, I would clarify that our interest is in the entire premises and not just the ground floor trading area. We find it essential for the proper control of a pub that the management and staff live above the premises and the yard at the back would also be required by the pub for it to operate without causing a nuisance to adjoining residents and to the locality.

Given the above we are certain that the premises can be run viably as a traditional public house serving the local community, as it has done over the last century or more, for the very long term.

Yours sincerely,

M R BUTLER

Seven potential buyers were bought to the table between December and February; the developer eventually put the Pineapple into an auction.

"My objections are as follows: – change of use would destroy an increasingly rare British institution, the socially integrated local pub. The Pineapple is the home of actuaries, actors, bricklayers, butchers, crooks, cabbies… Need I continue through the whole alphabet. In addition to its unique occupational mix it has always been racially mixed, and offered a pleasant place for women to drink without unwelcome attention. Most unusually, it is mixed in age terms. The young enjoying their first legal drink mix well with senior citizens. All this would be destroyed. […] – finally, and most importantly of all, change of use would rip the heart out of the community. I thought we were in the business of building communities – not destroying them". *GJ [obj141]*

Dear Mr Davies

"Whilst at the baby clinic this morning I was told about the closure of one of the nicest pubs in London – The Pineapple, Leverton Street. I suppose my pregnancy and my visit to hospital might explain why I had missed such a momentous event as the death of the landlord which is why I am late in pleading with the council not to give them planning permission for luxury flats to be developed at the site. It is not what we need in our neighbourhood to keep our community live and well. It is such a nice pub with a really good neighbourly feel to it. No underage drinkers and not rowdy but gentle and genuine in a way that one mostly sees on television nowadays […]" *JSM [obj134].*

"The Pineapple has a real warmth about it which comes not just from the actual surroundings but from the people who work there and the regulars who drink there. […six years ago] when I was trying to collect sponsors for my first London marathon, the landlady heard about it and asked that I leave one of my sponsor forms with her – within a couple of weeks she had raised £70 […]" *CM [obj302].*

"I am a resident of Falkland Road for some 18 years and although I am teetotal the loss of the Pineapple public house would be a devastating loss to the immediate area [...]" *JMM [obj174].*

Dear Mr Davies I have JUST discovered a gem of a pub on Monday night called 'The Pineapple'. It had everything I expect; good beer which was well kept, a traditional interior, friendly staff and peace and quiet. I was very disappointed to find it will be closing on 19 December, only to make way for flats and an office block. [...] I was very moved by the dedication and organisation with which the regulars have campaigned to save this pub. It is clear to me that it is more than a place to drink for these people. This is a traditional local pub which plays a large part in the life of its customers. It is a place that is open to the whole community to come to enjoy the facilities on offer [...] *CT [obj88].*

"**OH NO**, how dare you let the Pineapple close down; it's places like this that give London its character. Places like the Pineapple don't grow on trees you know!!!" *AF [obj358].*

'[...] I invite you to sample the atmosphere for yourself and I assure you, if you do, you will be writing one of these e-mails yourself'. *MB [obj255].*

INSIDE story

Name:
Terry Cooney
Job Title:
Principle Officer,
Budgets
Social Services

What does your job involve?

I'm in charge of Social Services' budgets - a total of £110 million a year. It's my job to make sure that we don't overspend and in nine years we never have - and that is probably unique for social services departments across the UK. There's a healthy friction between Finance and the rest of Social Services - we have to balance the books and this inevitably leads to a conflict between resources and care.

How long have you worked for Camden?

I have worked in the council for a total of 17 years and the last 9 years in Social Services.

What do you like most about your job?

There is always something exciting happening. As we move towards becoming part of the new Trust, I'm enjoying working with new colleagues in the NHS.

What do you like least about your job?

For the past few months, I have been doing two jobs because the Best Value Review said we needed to loose jobs and a member of the team went on maternity leave. Pressure has been high but they are now advertising for another member of staff.

Do you live in Camden?

Yes, in Kentish Town and I have four children ranging from 11 to 22 years old - and I can't persuade any of them to leave home: they love being in Camden too much.

What's your favourite thing about Camden?

Kentish Town's village feel. I'm proud of the campaign I was involved in to save my local pub, the Pineapple. It dates back to 1868 and was recently bought by a property developer. He had promised to maintain it as a pub but before the ink had even dried on the deal, he was planning to convert it into flats. Local residents swung into action to save the pub. We had the support of some really influential people: local actors, the newscaster Jon Snow and even Ken Livingstone (he used to be a member of Camden Council). We managed to get Grade II listing in just two days! The developer was almost in tears - and is now looking to sell.

How do you relax away from work?

I escape to my cottage in Kerry. There's Ireland's highest mountain in the back garden and the Atlantic Ocean outside the front door - and two pubs just 300 yards away.

DECEMBER

Mourners converge on Abbey Road studios to pay their respects to the former Beatle George Harrison. Below: The guitarist being painted by Patricia Angadi in late '60s.

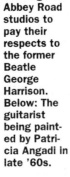

CAMDEN councillor Honora Morrissey provoked a war of words when she the crossed the chamber from the Tory group to the Liberal Democrats.

She claimed she was disillusioned with the Conservative party. Her former colleagues said she was only leaving because they had turned her down for her preferred seat at next May's council elections.

Beatles fans held a vigil outside Abbey Road studios as part of worldwide mourning for George Harrison, who died after a long battle with cancer.

Plans to refurbish Highgate Library, in Shepherd's Hill, were announced as part of preparations for its centenary celebrations.

Locals began a campaign to save the Pineapple pub in Kentish Town – a favourite haunt for famous actors – from being turned into homes.

Two brothers from Hampstead completed their transatlantic rowing challenge after 64 days at sea, having kept Ham&High readers up-to-date with their diary e-mailed along the way.

Camden police revealed plans to end round-the-clock opening at West Hampstead and Hampstead police stations.

After the auction the beer ran out – prompting three days of carry-in

Whispering repeatedly tackles his bike lock (from a sitting position); the bike falls on him

120 ...the last time the landlady persuades one of her regulars not to cycle home

...the crowd of onlookers continue to discuss with him the merits of cycling in 'his state'

Speeches were made

Songs were sung

The *Last Post* played

Call this a pub'

So the pub is in danger is it? Well, if Prince Charles has noticed, that means it must be — a man who goes into pubs so rarely that every time he does they take his photo.

The Prince of Wales says that the pub needs to diversify or die: he's right, pubs are under fierce attack and have been for years, though I have my doubts that diversification is the answer. Theme pubs to the left of us, wine bars to the right, lager, lager everywhere, nor anywhere decent to drink.

George Orwell famously defined the perfect pub in his essay The Moon Under Water. His ideal was somewhere where the barman knows your name and your usual, there's no music, and conversation flows as easily as the ale. Not somewhere where there are arsy bar staff, warm, bad, treacly chardonnay, and pumping beats called the Funky Snail or whatever focusgroup thinking deems fit.

Before I go any further, allow me to express an interest. For my sitcom — Time Gentlemen, Please

— we had found a great pub, the Admiral Blake, at the top of Ladbroke Grove in west London, to play the slightly run-down boozer needed. It was perfect, down to the graffitied walls, the tired green paint and fading signs. And then they did it up, repainted it, gave it the stripped-floor treatment. So it's personal, all right?

The thing is, similar unbroken pubs are being fixed all over. Why is this happening? It's our old friend, marketing, probably. Pubs aren't pubs — public houses — any more. They are retail outlets, floor space, alcopop/customer interfaces.

I have no objection to pubs making money, no objection to pubs serving decent food, but if they don't do either it really doesn't bother me. Now everything's stripped and themed, we're being taken for mugs, and mugged for the price of a packet of Kettle Chips.

I started drinking at school, in a pub called the Ship. It wasn't themed: that was its name. Okay,

SUNDAY TIME

126

? It's a theme park

there may have been a wheel over one of the fireplaces and one or two pictures of ships, but they didn't pretend that you were drinking on HMS Victory. They didn't even pretend it was a pub, because this was before things had got all self-conscious, and, either way, I was too busy trying to get semi-conscious to care.

But as we're treated to the ever-sickening glut of Irish pubs (been to Ireland? They just have pubs, you know, not Irish pubs), and the idea of merely going out, having a couple of drinks, enjoying the company of friends, has been re-packaged as something only the Irish can do properly. So the great British pub seems to have lost confidence in itself as more than just a thing that makes money, as a place of community, an end in itself, a hub.

By marketing us something we were already buying and maybe did not even know we were being sold, the marketing fraternity has sold us all down the river for a handful of designer pistachio nuts.

Surely pubs are not and cannot be just retail space. The moment we start thinking like this the next thing you know good local boozers will be shut down and end up being turned into offices. In fact it is already happening — this month saw the residents of Kentish Town in north London launch a campaign to save their local, the Pineapple, from property developers who want to convert the neighbourhood's prime asset into office space.

For my money, pubs are like trains — they are for getting to and from work. Sometimes in the afternoon there are only three people in them, and they might smell a bit, but that's fine. And like trains they don't seem to go to the country any more.

Now that may not matter to some urban types, but a friend of mine has just moved out of a pub-less village he lived in for five years. The damage to his personal life has been catastrophic.

To cut a long story short, he ended up singing in choirs, and

even got out his battered French horn to parp away aimlessly in some local school orchestra, just so he could meet people. The next thing he knew he was going on blind dates with women he had met on the phone. I blame a brewery, but I'm not sure which one, probably Ind Coope.

The village I grew up in had two pubs, the Swan and the Carpenters Arms — normal pubs, not gastro, not wine bars. Never have pubs been more normal. In terms of their impact on village life they were busier than the two churches — as well as offering a better range of bar snacks.

While the pub may or may not be the hub, it's certainly something to do in isolated, busless rural Britain. Margaret Thatcher was right, there is no such thing as society. But there are pubs, and they're the next best thing.

Al Murray

Time Gentlemen, Please is on Sky One tomorrow at 10pm

23/12/2001

LETTERS

Write to protest about plans for great pub

Help us keep the Pineapple

❏ IN a week when the Prince of Wales launched a campaign to stop the decline in village pubs we are faced with a proposal for the closure of the inestimable Pineapple in Leverton Street, and its conversion to residential units.

This would be a huge loss to the hundreds of locals who use the pub like a social centre and who rely on the welcome, the conversation, the support and friendship it provides.

Charles's The Pub is the Hub applies equally to the many small communities that make up any city.

In our bit of Kentish

Celebrity protesters: (from left) actors Michael Garner and Ken Stott, newsreader Jon Snow and actor roger Lloyd Pack

Town we have watched four pubs disappear in as many years all for residential conversion. Pubs are community resources. People meet each other in them, catch up on local news, offer help to those going through illness or hard times and discuss neighbourhood issues that affect them all.

Any local authority planning guidance needs to reflect the importance of these vital community resources. Pubs like the Pineapple should have a protected status in Camden's Unitary Development Plan. At the moment they don't.

If you don't want to see the Pineapple or your local, go the way of so many in Camden, write to the planners now to refuse the change of use (ref PEX0100941) and to incorporate protection of pubs into the UDP.

The Pineapple may serve alcohol, but the spirit which the regulars cherish is that of community.

SUE PRICKETT
Chair
Leighton Road
Neighbourhood Association
NW5

Developers withdraw plans for Pineapple

THE buyers of the Pineapple pub in Kentish Town have withdrawn their application to convert it into luxury housing, the Ham&High learned on Monday.

The news came only days after the pub closed – with regulars vowing to continue the fight to save their local.

Drinkers had mounted a vigorous campaign to oppose the proposals after Crossier Properties Ltd sought planning permission to convert the Victorian pub into flats and office space.

The pub, in Leverton Street, is a favourite of star actors, including Roger Lloyd Pack, Ken Stott and Rufus Sewell. TV newsreader Jon Snow is also a regular.

Mr Stott was among the drinkers who turned out for the final night on Wednesday last week when an auction of Pineapple memorabilia was held, raising £850 for a "fighting fund". Among the items that went under the hammer was an 1868 bell, used to call time, which fetched £250.

Regulars are now concerned that the pub might fall prey to vandals while it is unoccupied and are mobilising a neighbourhood watch scheme.

❏ See Comment, page 12.

Regulars at the Pineapple in Kentish Town help raise £850 for a fighting fund to keep the pub open. Back row: Colm Kelly, Tony Davis, Gill Scott and Mike Babb. Front row: Ali Watt, Kate Burgin and Sarah Cooper. Picture by Luke Williamson

Website Address: http://www.camden.gov.uk/planning
Email Address: env.devcon@camden.gov.uk

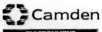

ENVIRONMENT

Enquiries to: Mr J. Davies
Tel.No.: 0207 974 5885

Development Control
Planning Services
London Borough of Camden
Town Hall
Your Ref:
Our Ref: PEX0100941
Date: 21st December 2001

Argyle Street
London WC1H 8ND

Tel 020 7278 4444
Fax 020 7974 1975

Gavin Darwell-Taylor
Axia Architects
Unit 1
9A Dallington Street
Clerkenwell
London EC1V OBQ

Dear Mr Darwell-Taylor,

Town and Country Planning Act 1990
Planning,Listed Buildings and Conservation Areas Act 1990
Re: The Pineapple Public House, 51 Leverton Street, NW5

I refer to your planning application for the change of use and conversion of the above
public house to provide 4 residential units including a roof extension together with the
erection of a 2 storey building at the rear fronting Railey Mews for separate office use
(Class B1).

As you are aware the property has recently been statutorily Listed as being of special
architectural or historic interest (Grade II). This has very important implications for your
proposals as the listing protects both the exterior and interior of the building. In view of the
impending holiday break and recent closure of the pub, I am writing to set out my views on
your proposals and my advice in respect of acceptable works to a listed building.

The property is referred to in the listing description as "an unusually exuberant example of a
mid-Victorian pub" and specific reference is made to bar features on the ground floor. These
features must be retained intact together with other architectural elements such as cornices,
paneling, etc. which contribute to its character. I feel therefore, that in line with UDP policy
EN39 which covers the use of listed buildings, the ground floor and associated basement
storage areas must be retained for use as a public house or similar use. With regard to the
upper floors, these have been used as residential accommodation ancillary to the public house
with access from a central staircase behind the bar. I consider that this accommodation
should remain in such use as I consider it would not be possible to self-contain the upper
floors without compromising the plan form , character and use of the ground floor as a pub.

The proposed roof extension needs to be considered both in the light of roof extension policy
in the UDP (EN24) and its impact on the listed building (EN38). The property is in a terrace
where there are very few roof extensions and it has a prominent position closing the vista
from Ascham Street. In these circumstances I consider that the principle of a roof extension is
unacceptable as it would be unduly prominent on the building and disrupt the roofline of the
terrace.

The proposed rear extension in Railey Mews for office use would create a two storey
building along the backs of Leverton Street properties where as existing only walls and single

Director Peter Bishop

INVESTOR IN PEOPLE

storey structures exist. The extension would be unduly prominent and would detract from the existing scale and character of the Mews. I consider therefore that it is not acceptable.

I consider that it is in the best interests of the building that it be brought back into use as soon as possible and to avoid a period of vacancy. It is very important that no works are carried out to the interior or exterior without the written approval of the Council and that the building is properly secured to prevent unlawful entry by squatters, vandals, etc. I would remind you that as owner of the building you are responsible for its security and it is a criminal offence to carry out unlawful works to a listed building.

I am minded to refuse your application on the above grounds unless you confirm that you wish to withdraw it.

Yours faithfully

John Davies
Senior Planner
for Director, Environment Department

cc. Crossier Properties – Mr Sohail Sarbuland

LONDON BOROUGH OF CAMDEN
ENVIRONMENT DEPARTMENT -
DEVELOPMENT CONTROL
This is to formally notify the public that two applications for planning permission have been formally withdrawn by the applicants.
These are : -
(1) 1-11 Swains Lane and garages, 109-110 Highgate West Hill and garages, N6 (Ref. No. PEX0100720). "Demolition of garages and ground floor units fronting both Highgate West Hill and Swains Lane and the redevelopment of the site to provide a part three/part four storey development, comprising five commercial units at ground floor level and 18 residential units above".
This application was withdrawn by the applicant on the 3rd December 2001.
(2) Pineapple Public House, 51 Leverton Street, NW1 (Ref. No: PEX0100941). "Change of use of former public house and mansard roof extension to provide 3 maisonettes and one flat. New structure at rear facing Railey Mews comprising an office unit (Class B1) with car parking space".
This application was withdrawn by the applicant on the 21st December 2001.

Hope for pub as developers drop

Pineapple st

ticks around

by DAN CARRIER

THE saga of the pub that would not close took a twist over Christmas when the new owners failed to complete the deal to buy the building.

Regulars at the Pineapple pub in Leverton Street, Kentish Town, refused to let their favourite watering hole go quietly after it was bought by developers following the death of publican Sean Gately in November.

The pub was sold to Crossier Ltd at a knockdown price on the understanding it would stay open. But days after making the verbal agreement to keep the pub and redevelop upstairs, developers put in a new application to turn it in to a series of yuppie flats.

But they failed to pay the balance of the fee and are now days away from reneging on the £500,000 deal.

And campaigners were pleased to hear that the first battle to save the historic pub has been won. Jonty Boyce, who has co-ordinated the campaign, said: "We do not know why the developers failed to complete but it may be because the financiers withdrew their offer.

"They still could complete the sale and put a new design in. But their stalling looks like it is down to the fact the pub has been listed and also because of the strength of public opinion."

The Gately family, who have run the pub since 1987, had a Christmas in limbo. Their furniture had gone to their new home – but they were unable to follow it because of the developers stalling.

Big-hearted regulars stepped in to make sure their Christmas was not miserable – a whip round bought £125 of Christmas cheer from a top food store. They opened the pub on Christmas Day and New Year's Day for locals – who had to bring their own booze because the pub has officially closed and had no beer or spirits left.

Mr Boyce added: "We may come to the end of this quickly. The developers may see sense and sell it someone who will run it as a pub but otherwise we are in for a long and hard campaign. We will fight to the bitter end to save this important building."

Days before Christmas the new owners found out that locals had applied for the Victorian building to be given Grade Two listed status, putting more obstacles in the way of turning them into luxury flats.

A spokesman for the owners, who have until January 9 to complete the deal, declined to comment.

Pictured: Locals celebrate the good news at a special New Year's Day party at their favourite watering hole.

The very last orders

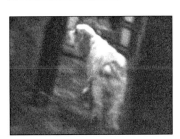

Regulars hope to pull in buyers to save pub

REGULARS of the threatened Pineapple pub are so keen to reopen it they are meeting potential buyers to drum up interest in the business.

The last pint was pulled at the pub in Leverton Street, Kentish Town, on December 16 but locals, including Channel 4 newsreader Jon Snow and actor Rufus Sewell, have not called time on their campaign to save it.

Campaigners have already forced owners Crossier Properties Ltd to withdraw an application to convert it into flats and offices by getting English Heritage to grant the pub a Grade II listing.

The firm finally clinched the £500,000 sale of the pub on January 8 but is said to be planning to sell it on.

Gill Scott, of Pineapple Rescue, said: "We have been trying to find, and help, potential buyers who want to reopen the premises as a pub. We are realistically informing interested parties about past takings and what a good backstreet local it really was.

"We have spoken to two or three people who seem quite interested and we know that offers have been made. The new owners have now told us to send any potential buyers to them."

7 potential buyers

The developer, Sohail Sarbuland of Crossier Properties, considered he had purchased a development opportunity [for £500,000]; he had already bought, closed and changed to residential use a pub in Roman Road. The listing meant that he now had no hope of creating his four flats and offices in the Pineapple but he wanted a large profit. As a pub, a going concern, it was considered to be worth between £500,000 and £560,000.

In December 2001 CAMRA knew about 13 pubs, all located in villages, that had been bought and run by groups of locals; two were owned by Parish Councils. For locals to buy a pub from a developer, especially at city prices, would be almost impossible.

Hoping to bring the pub back into use the committee continued to bring serious buyers to the table. But our campaign had also raised the stakes; Sohail was advised that he would make more money at auction and rejected all offers from brewers, beer cooperatives, publicans, and committed friends of the pub. The Pineapple was put into a residential auction catalogue, advertised as having *'potential for residential development subject to all necessary consents'*. Having overheard '...would make a lovely studio and you can always get round the planners' the viewings were picketed in order to tell potential buyers of the listed status; campaign posters were torn down by the agents.

The Pineapple sold before the auction for £680,000.

Drinkers are all set to celebrate after pub rescue

REGULARS from a historic pub which was closed in December are getting ready to toast its re-opening.

The Pineapple Pub in Leverton Street, Kentish Town, was sold last year to developers who planned to turn it into flats.

But furious drinkers formed the "Pineapple Rescue" campaign, and persuaded English Heritage to grant the building listed status – meaning the building cannot be altered.

Even so, The Pineapple still had to be shut down while a new buyer was sought – leaving regulars in limbo without a pub.

Gill Scott, of the Pineapple Rescue campaign said: "It's been closed for a month now but everyone's still keeping in contact.

"There's an e-mail newsletter which goes out to 300 former Pineapple regulars.

"People have even gone out and bought mobile phones just so they can stay in touch.

"We have met up in various other pubs around Kentish Town – but it's just not the same."

Developers Crossier have apparently already received

By **CAROLINE RYDER**

several enquiries from potential buyers.

Campigners are hoping for a quick sale so the pub can re-open sooner rather than later.

Campaigner Dr Jonty Boyce said: "It would very, very expensive for the new owner just to sit on it for a year.

"Plus the council would probably put pressure on them to do something if it was just being left empty. When it does re-open, there's going to be one hell of a party."

Pineapple deal a 'victory'

by DAN CARRIER

DEVELOPERS buying the Pineapple pub in Leverton Street, Kentish Town, have finally completed the sale – but campaigners trying to stop them turning the Victorian grade two listed building into yuppie flats are calling their protests a success.

Crossier Ltd completed the deal at the last minute – they had until January 9 to finalise the sale but had dragged their heels finding the cash after paying a deposit of £50,000.

But on the last day before the sale would have fallen through, the company found the £450,000 balance.

But campaigners believe the strength of public opinion has made the developers change their plans.

A concerted campaign to keep the pub as it is has pulled in a host of local celebrities, including Jon Snow of Channel Four News, actors Rufus Sewell and Roger Lloyd-Pack.

Now campaign organiser Jonty Boyce said he was confident the developers would sell on the property to a company that wants to re-open it.

He told the New Journal: "We think the buyer is going to try and sell so we want an interested publican to buy it and run it as the Pineapple pub."

A source at the developers told campaigners that because of the strength of public opinion the new owners had got cold feet over the yuppie flats deal.

Mr Boyce continued: "Crossier now seem to accept that their option to develop is pretty much over. We are obviously pleased about this, but we will only be really happy when it is open again and we can go and have a pint there."

But currently the only visitors at the bar is the 24-hour security guard who is looking after the property for the new owners.

Mr Boyce said he was "not counting my chickens – but I have it on good authority it will be sold on as a pub."

Saving the Pineapple, NW5

Mark Hoile reports on details of this important local campaign

This issue of The Full Pint brings news of a tense and fast moving story that began in the quiet residential streets of Kentish Town, and is to this day is still a burning issue at the heart of the local community.

The Pineapple in Leverton Street NW5, nestles amongst rows of well presented urban terraces, well away from the noisy and congested main routes of the surrounding area. It has been a home to the community for over 100 years, attracting a friendly and relaxed clientele who at times have even possessed their own door keys to the pub!

A family run Victorian free house, the pub was placed on the market by the widow of the late landlord Sean Gately. An early purchase was agreed with a property developer based on an understanding that the ground floor pub would be preserved as a going concern, with the upper floors renovated and converted to residential flats. However following the completion of the sale, a further party submitted new plans to redevelop the whole site into maisonettes and a new office, with the total loss of the pub. The departing family of the late landlord who have a strong attachment to both the pub and its customers then realised that they had been misled.

This news met an immediate response from the pub regulars who came together to create a dynamic and well-managed campaign group to save their local. The campaign committee quickly called a public meeting at a nearby church hall (above), attended by more than fifty interested people. This allowed a strategy to be developed calling on the resources available within those supporters who had joined the fight. Additional support came from North London CAMRA,

Pub Preservation
The Pineapple, NW5

and The London Pubs Group. The Pineapple campaign then rallied further support from London Mayor Ken Livingstone, and other notable public figures. Media interest was generated with main articles appearing in the Lon-

don Evening Standard (13th December 2001), The Camden New Journal (13th December 2001), and on local radio.

Throughout early December each day became a race against time with the pub scheduled to finally close its doors on December 16th. However the first fruits of the protesters' efforts began to show when the full sanction of the mortgage to the new owners was delayed, when the pub was given a Grade II listed status by English Heritage. This action was the result of a submission by campaigners, which included a comprehensive set of specially commissioned professional photographs. A decision by the landlord's family then kept the pub open for a further three days as more beer had been delivered, and had to be drunk! This further raised the community spirit. The submission to English Heritage had revealed that the pub had a long and hidden history

exhibiting many period features and had at one time been a butcher's shop with some fixtures still visible in the cellar today.

In advance of the final closure the campaign group organised an auction of all the removable wall mountings from the bar area. This raised £2000 for the fighting fund, with the intention that buyers keep the items in their own homes until the pub fully reopens, when they will once again be restored to the walls of the bar.

Whilst the pub remains shut (with a resident security guard) the campaign is stimulating the interest of local publicans and breweries for a potential resale and reopening as a public house early in 2002. The Pineapple is a superb example of the

power of public protest and organised campaigning, when faced with the loss of both a public amenity and historical pub.

The Pineapple campaign group welcome support from all interested parties and can be contacted via the Full Pint, with further developments to be reported in the next issue. In the meantime, an information display will be available at London Drinker Beer Festival.

An array of Good Beer Guide stickers in the window of the Pineapple.

Pineapple back on the market as developers told flats not an option

by DAN CARRIER

A GRADE II-listed pub which was closed last month after being bought by property speculators have been put back on the market.

Locals of the Pineapple Pub in Leverton Street, Kentish Town, which included actor Roger Lloyd Pack and newsreader Jon Snow, had campaigned against the pub's closure but were unable to prevent it.

But now Camden planners have told the developers unofficially that preliminary drawings showing plans to turn the popular watering hole into yuppie flats would never be approved.

The Pineapple closed last December after publican Sean Gately died. It was bought up by a Holborn-based property speculator's Crossier Ltd. who, after purchasing the pub at a knockdown price on the understanding that they would keep it open, sacked the staff and shut regulars out.

They announced plans to build exclusive flats and a set of offices in the courtyard – which kickstarted a massive public campaign to keep it open.

But just two months after the firm bought the pub, they have admitted defeat – but still, according to sources, hope to sell the pub at a profit to another developer, who could then resurrect plans to convert the 1870 building into luxury housing.

Jonty Boyce, spokesman for the campaign to save the pub, said he hoped anyone bidding for the pub would see sense. He said: "In essence the council have vetoed putting in any residential developments in the building – but we are not sure anyone bidding for it will know this."

The building has been placed in a residential sale, due to take place on March 25 at the Café Royal in Regent Street.

He said regulars would go to the auction to warn people that it was not appropriate for development.

He said: "It would be very foolish for any one to buy it with the idea of turning it into posh houses. If they do, they will just get their fingers burnt. It was a great local pub – and it will be a great local pub again."

Crossier Ltd, who have refused to talk to the New Journal since they bought the pub, declined to comment.

'The Pineapple Pub', 51 Leverton Street, Kentish Town, London NW5

**A Freehold Well Located Grade II Listed
End of Terrace Former Public House.
Potential for Residential Development subject to all
necessary consents**

LOT
139

Full Vacant Possession upon Completion

Front of 51 Leverton Street

Rear of 51 Leverton Street

The Property
Crown Copyright Reserved

The Property

The above plan is for identification purposes only.
See paragraph 2 of Notices to Prospective Purchasers
contained within the Auction Catalogue.

Tenure
Freehold.

Location
Leverton Street is located off Leighton Road, which in turn runs off Kentish Town Road. The property is situated on the west side of Leverton Street, at its junction with Railey Mews. Extensive shops and amenities, including Kentish Town Rail and Northern Line Underground Station, are available with the further shops and restaurants of Camden and Highgate being within reach.

Description
The property comprises an end of terrace former public house arranged over ground and two upper floors. The property benefits from a rear beer garden with access onto Railey Mews and an external workshop.

Accommodation

Ground Floor
Bar Area through to Darts Room
Ladies' and Gentlemans' WCs
Further Gents' Urinals
Access to Cellar Area

First Floor
Front Room
Further Room
Kitchen

Half Landing
Separate WC and wash basin

Second Floor
Three Rooms
Bathroom with wash basin
and WC (Large)

Planning
Local Planning Authority: London Borough of Camden.
Tel: 020 7278 4444.

The property offers potential for residential development subject to all necessary consents.

Viewing
The property will be open for viewing every Tuesday before the Auction between 11.30 a.m. – 12 noon (Ref: RA).
Vendor's Solicitor Solomon Taylor & Shaw (Ref: SA). Tel: 020 7431 1912 Fax: 020 7794 7485

VACANT – Freehold Former Public House

LONDON – M25

64

Enquiries to: Mr J. Davies
Tel.No.: 0207 974 5885

Your Ref: Lot 139/Auction on 25th March
Our Ref:
Date: 15th March 2002

R.Adamson Esq
Allsop
100 Knights bridge
London
SW1X 7LB

Dear Mr Adamson,

Town and Country Planning Act 1990
Re: The Pineapple Public House, 51 Leverton Street, NW5

I refer to your sale particulars for the residential auction on the 25th March 2002 concerning the above site, which is numbered Lot 139.

I have concerns over your representation of the site as having *"potential for residential development subject to all necessary consents"* as it is Camden Planning officers' view that the building should continue in use as a public house in the interests of preserving its special architectural and historic interest as a Grade II listed building. Planning and listed building consent would be unlikely to be granted for a total conversion to residential use and indeed, given the nature of the building, it is unlikely that even a partial conversion to independent residential use would be accepted.

To assist potential bidders an informal guidance note has been prepared by officers giving advice on how the building might be used/extended/altered. **Please bring this to potential bidders attention.**

The property has a lawful use as pub on the basement and ground floors with associated residential accommodation on the 1st and 2nd floors. The whole property therefore has A3 use rights. Continued use for purposes within Class A3 will not require planning permission. Self-containment of the upper floors into separate residential use will require planning permission.

Informal Officer Guidelines:

Roof extensions likely to be unacceptable as the property retains an original butterfly roof and rear parapet in largely unspoilt roof line. There are prominent views of premises along Leverton Street and Ascham Street.

Rear extensions likely to be unacceptable above ground floor level as there are very few in terrace and back of the terrace is highly visible from Railey Mews to the rear and side. Some scope for rationalisation of the existing rear ground floor additions subject to retention of 50% of rear un-built on.

Ground floor- bar areas including fireplaces and decorative plasterwork of considerable importance and noted in Listing description-to be retained as existing. There are opportunities to rationalise the plan towards the rear (19th century and 20th century additions). The WCs are not of intrinsic value. Where it is proposed to remove partitions, the loss of original, structural walls would be resisted. The removal of outbuildings at the rear is acceptable in principle, since they mostly comprise 20th century *ad hoc* additions of no architectural value.

First Floor- a principal floor within the listed building which retains its original plan form and consists of a large room at the front and two small rooms at the rear, either side of a central staircase. Front room has decorative ceiling plasterwork and a sizeable chimney piece on the north wall. Retain fireplace in rear room. Resist alterations to the plan form.

Second Floor- the plan form and original features (including fireplaces) should be retained as far as possible.

External alterations- existing prominent front and side elevations to be retained as existing including fenestration pattern and materials and especially the 'pineapple' decorations. Keep 'Pineapple' name if possible.

Ventilation duct- the existing property has no cooking facilities part from domestic kitchen and therefore the creation of a commercial kitchen associated with pub food or restaurant is likely to require mechanical ventilation. Approval for external ducting unlikely to be given and consideration needs to be given to internal ventilation using existing flues.

General Views
In listed building terms, it would be most appropriate to keep the building in its present form, avoiding alterations to the plan form and negative impact on historic features. The optimum solution would therefore be to retain the listed building in its current use as a public house at ground floor (and basement) and ancillary residential use at first and second floor levels.

I trust the above advice is helpful and further advice or clarification can be provided on request.

The planning advice contained in this letter is informal and without prejudice to the determination of any subsequent planning or listed building application.

Yours Sincerely,

John Davies
Senior Planner
for Director, Environment Department

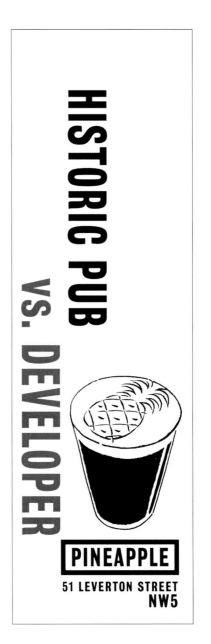

**Positive developments at Pineapple
as victory beckons for locked-out regulars
of Kentish Town pub**

IF IT'S WORTH IT FIGHT FOR IT

Some of you may know the Pineapple in Leverton Street, Kentish Town, while others may have read about the campaign to save the currently closed local from property developers – three months of intense action that seems likely at last to be succeeding in its aim of scuppering proposals for yuppie flats where dartboards, bar-stools and beer barrels ought to be.

Fifteen pubs have fallen to the property developers in the vicinity in the past couple of years. Of course, some of them have been sold as a result of business failure, and some are less than popular with nearby residents, in which case few will lament their passing. But when even such a thriving and highly regarded boozer as the Pineapple can come under mortal threat, it is clear that this is a danger all local pub regulars may have to face.

Promising to reopen it soon as a pub, someone has just bought the Pineapple from the thwarted developers. Although there is many a slip twixt the mug and the lip, here are a few of the reasons why the campaign looks like bearing fruit and the regulars may resume their places at the bar after a quarter-of-a-year gap and doubtless say: *"It was your round when the pub shut, now get them in."*

 Organisation and mobilisation. As soon as there is a whiff of such a crisis, regulars need to form a committee, allocate tasks, pool expertise and bring together those with specific talents. Does your pub have regulars who may be lawyers, graphic designers, journalists? And celebrities among the clientele can come in handy for publicity purposes. A planning-policy expert is a rare bonus. Contact CAMRA!

 Lobby the planners. Every letter and email with an address counts; letters from Community groups carry great weight. Camden Council were reportedly stunned by the number of communications received in support of the Pineapple Rescue campaign. Tireless work lay behind the 533 messages received.

 Speed is of the essence. Things can happen very quickly in the property game, so the response must be immediate. This might allow the pub to be listed before anything can happen to the premises (as crucially happened at the now Grade II Pineapple) and it makes clear to buyers and developers that they have a fight on their hands.

 Media matters. Get the press onside – the Pineapple was extensively covered in national newspapers and on Radio 4, and the local papers were especially helpful.

 Maintain pressure. Be relentless in your opposition. Make would-be developers aware that your people are not going away.

 Be pro-active. Do you know anyone who would step in and run this pub of yours? Bring someone to the table with the property men.

If all fails, and your pub does shut down, you could always drop in at the Pineapple – where you are sure to get a sympathetic ear.
                                        We've been there.

148

	Skirmish diary
06.12.2001 ●	**planning application notice found**
07.12.2001	**acquired copies of plans**
	first meeting of committee 9 pm
08.12.2001	produced posters, flyers, banner for pub
09.12.2001	**meeting of committee Mick Lewis [CAMRA] attended**
10.12.2001	building photo shoot, requested listing
	press releases
12.12.2001	**public meeting**
13.12.2001	press, radio
15.12.2001	**produced T-shirts**
16.12.2001	leafleted Sunday newspapers
18.12.2001 ●	**Pineapple LISTED**
19.12.2001	memorabilia auction
●	**pub CLOSED**
20.12.2001	**Campaign submission against planning application**
	Camden officers visited the pub
21.12.2001	Camden wrote to architects
	architects withdrew application
	property company lost loan
	developer failed to complete
	family had to stay in pub, empty of furniture
25.12.2001	**Christmas Day carry-in**
01.01.2002	New Year's Day carry-in
06.01.2002	**Gately Pineapple's last carry-in party**
	Mehmet's shop suffering big losses
07.01.2002	locals secured pub against break-in
08.01.2002 ●	**property developer COMPLETED purchase**
17.01.2002	produced badges
	Radio 4: *You and yours* interview
08.03.2002	**developer plans to auction pub 25 March**
	more CAMRA advice
11.03.2002	auction catalogue published
	committee wrote to Camden, auctioneers
	produced literature for potential bidders
12.03.2002	**committee picketed viewings**
15.03.2002	Camden wrote to auctioneers
	OFFER for pub accepted [prior to auction]
20.03.2002	**CAMRA festival, Bidborough Street**
23.03.2002	new owners put in plans for:
	reduced size bar and a backpackers' hostel
	invited to withdraw by Camden
26.03.2002	**committee met new owners to tell of campaign,**
	character and economic success of back street pub
10.04.2002 ●	**new owners COMPLETED on purchase**
	renovations began immediately
16.05.2002 ●	**PINEAPPLE REOPENED**
10.06.2002	retrospective planning application for
	works already carried out, including:
	halving the size of the cellars
	bringing the function room into use as a restaurant
	application also included putting the toilets
	in the basement [which did not happen]
	permission granted 17.01.2003
01.08.2002	planning application for a conservatory
	permission granted 19.08.2003

12 DAYS
SAVING THE FABRIC

126 DAYS
WRESTLING with DEVELOPER

LOCALS CELEBRATE AS PINEAPPLE STAYS A PUB

Left to right: Pineapple regulars with campaign organisers Jon Budd, Sue Hunter, Gill Scott and Jonty Boyce

THE Pineapple pub in Leverton Street, Kentish Town, has been saved from redevelopment – just days before it was due to be auctioned off and turned into yuppie flats.

Sources close to the campaign to save the pub told the New Journal a well-known local family called the Powells – who it is believed have a history in running successful local pubs – have stepped in to safeguard the historic watering hole.

The developers bought the pub in December from the Gately family, who have run the pub for 15 years, and have finally admitted defeat in their attempts to turn the pub in to posh flats.

The mysterious figure behind the sale – known only as Mr Saburland, head of Crossier Ltd – has consistently refused to talk to the press about the future of the popular watering hole.

When news of the closure first broke, regulars who included Channel Four newsreader Jon Snow and actor Roger Lloyd Pack launched a campaign to save it.

But Mr Saburland confirmed reports that the pub had been sold. He said: "We have sold it on to a pub operator."

He would not reveal how much he sold it for.

Sources at the pub revealed that it was originally sold for around £500,000 as a going concern, before the developers decided to turn it into yuppie flats and build offices in the back courtyard.

Sources say Crossier – who could have got more than £1m at auction for the Grade II listed pub, dating from 1870 – would have received a substantial increase in their outlay, and rumours among campaigners say the developers could have earned over £100,000 in profit for the six weeks they owned the pub.

Regular Jonty Boyce, who led a massive public campaign to keep the pub open, told the New Journal it was an incredible victory.

He said: "It has been sold to a father and daughter who live locally and will open it up again, as it was, in partnership.

You always hear these stories of developers getting their own way – but this story has a happy ending. We are absolutely thrilled – this is a victory for the common man, for the community, and for keeping this little part of Kentish Town alive."

THEY DRINK IT'S ALL OVER!

IN BRIEF

Pineapple will stay pub

DRINKERS have won their battle to save The Pineapple, the "luvvies' pub" in Kentish Town.

Developer Crossier Properties Ltd, which had bought the pub to turn it into flats and offices, gave in to months of "people power" and sold it last week to Francis Powell and his daughter Chloë Powell.

Ms Powell intends to run the Grade II-listed building as a pub with the backing of her father.

The watering hole in Leverton Street, which was due to be auctioned on March 25, was bought by the Powells last Tuesday.

Dr Jonty Boyce, 51, a stalwart of the campaign, said: "The developers have been forced to back down by people power. The pub will probably re-open in the next three months."

On Wednesday, members of the Pineapple Rescue Committee appeared at a beer festival at the Camden Centre, in Bidborough Street, on a stall showcasing the stories of less fortunate pubs that were closed by developers.

The number of pubs 'saved' by 2001 was fewer than 20; in the last ten years (up to 2011) the number 'saved' is still in the twenties. Very few pubs (one!) have been 'saved by a campaign' after being sold to a developer.

*In 2001 there were about 60,500 pubs in UK with two pubs a week closing; by 2011 there were 52,000 pubs with 25 a week closing [British Beer & Pub Association]. London was the biggest loser of pubs – with five a week, and 276 a year. Sohail and Crossier Properties went on to buy and close several more pubs. **The Pineapple lives.***

152 Photocall for the renewed Pineapple

154 *They drink. It's all over!* Opening night of the Powell era

Sue Gyford

Pub's

their l

Local causes ta
of the Pineapple

PROTESTERS who helped save Kentish Town's Pineapple pub are to donate leftover campaign funds to local charities.

Organisers have declared the Pineapple Rescue Campaign officially over and say they are satisfied the Grade II-listed pub is safe in the hands of its new landlords.

The campaign was launched in December 2001 after developers Crossier Properties bought the pub in Leverton Street and asked Camden Council for permission to turn it into flats and offices.

Regulars, including newsreader Jon Snow and actors Rufus Sewell and Roger Lloyd Pack, joined the fight. Crossier Properties eventually bowed to public pressure and agreed to sell the Pineapple to father and daughter team, Francis and Chloë Powell.

The campaign's Jonty Bloom told the Ham&High: "We're extremely pleased with the way it's gone. There's still the wider issue, which is that back-street pubs where the residential value exceeds the commercial value are always going to be under threat in this way unless the council protects them. Other councils do protect them but Camden doesn't appear to be interested."

The remaining £1,000 donated to the campaign by well-wishers will now be split between three local organisations.

Flapjacks café, in Kentish Town Road, which offers employment and work experience to people with learning difficulties, will receive £475. Project manager Suzanne Hovells said: "It's brilliant. Things like this don't happen very often and when they do it's wonderful. The best idea we've

come up with is to buy a new till. It would benefit everybody if our trainees could use a till that has pictures on instead of numbers."

Volunteer Reading Help, which trains volunteers to help children in local primary schools learn to read, and a Christmas food hamper campaign for the needy will also benefit.

Campaign members will donate the so-called "Pineapple archive" of papers and photographs documenting their fight to the Camden Local Studies and Archive Centre at Holborn library.

The Pineapple closed after landlord Sean Gateley died in December 2001. When his widow, Mary, sold the building to Crossier Properties she said she had done so on the basis it would be kept as a pub – as it had been for 133 years.

Locals bombarded their councillors, London Mayor Ken Livingstone and even the Home Secretary with 500 letters of protest and interviewed potential landlords themselves to try to interest them in running the pub.

When the pumps finally ran dry in January the campaign even

saviours donate
eftovers to charity

aste generosity
e campaigners

**The Pineapple in Kentish Town
and (right) some of the pub
faithfuls who helped save it.**

bought enough bottles of beer to
put off its closure by three days.

As well as eventually securing
its future as a pub, they persuaded
English Heritage to protect the
Pineapple with a Grade II listing.
Francis and Chloë Powell
reopened it last May and have set
up a restaurant on the first floor.

sue.gyford@hamhigh.co.uk

158 *Pineapple diaspora at Jorene Celeste*, **Bob Gibson** 2007

This book is dedicated to all those who made the Pineapple what it was and to all those who decided to do something to *save* it. If you are amongst the people 'snapped' on these pages I hope you will be happy to be recorded here; the photographs were offered by *regulars* and *activists,* orchestrated by Gill Scott.

Special thanks will always be due to the late Michael Balfour who found the Planning Advice notice and galvanised us all into action; to those at English Heritage who acted with amazing speed; to Mike Babb, Jonty Boyce, Jon Budd, Paul Chinnery, Tim Cooper, Mehmet Dilloo, Martin James, Nick Hinton, Imogen and Simon Holmes, Sue Hunter, Elisabeth Ingles, James Maskell, Robert Palmer, Bettina Schmid, Gill Scott, Tanya Shillingford, Ali Watt, Alex Williams, George DeVille; to CAMRA advisers Mark Hoile, Jane Jephcote, Mike Lewis, Iain Loe; to the 533 individuals who cared enough to write letters and emails to the Planners at the council; to Jim Robins [drawing of Pine-Guinness]; to Richard Leeney [photographer]; to Sodge at Fifth Column [printing nearly 200 T-shirts the sale of which raised £1,399]; all of you who bought memorabilia at the auction – raising £1,056.80; to the 'stars' and the newspapers who gave us the oxygen of publicity, and to TV and radio who broadcast the story; to Malcolm Holmes [archivist]; to the seven publicans, brewers and interested investors who attempted to wrest the pub from the developer by buying it; to Desmond Paul [security]; to Jem and Ben whose offer of a fund-raising gig was never able to be taken up and to Paul Shearsmith who played *The last post* as we left on 6 January 2002.

Acknowledgments: **Images supplied** from the collections of Michael Balfour and Elisabeth Ingles, Jonty Boyce [including video clips], Mandy Callender, Michael Fletcher, Christine Gately, Mike Hollis, Imogen and Simon Holmes, Freddie Prior, Gill Scott, Julia Vezza and George DeVille. **Anecdotes** recounted by Mike Babb, Mandy Callender, John Charlton, Tony Davis, Christine Gately, Mary Gately, Mike Hollis, Imogen and Simon Holmes, Elisabeth Ingles, Dylan (Mogsi) Morris, Gwilym (Bert) Owen, Pat Purcell (Nice), Gill Scott, Wynne Thomas, Julia Vezza, Ali Watt, Brian (Whispering) Williams. **Editing** by the consummate professional: Elisabeth Ingles. **Extracts** from some of the 533 letters sent to the Planning department of Camden Council in December 2001 are from the copies which are now held in the Camden Local Studies and Archives Centre [Holborn Library] under reference number ACC01152 [together with the newspaper cuttings].

The developer paid £500,000 for the Pineapple and sold it for £680,000 three months later. The Pineapplers could never afford to buy the pub; they did raise money to run a campaign. *Camden New Journal* Christmas appeal, The Camden Society and Eleanor Palmer Volunteer Reading Help scheme each received £475.75 as a division of the remaining funds in December 2002.

Produced and published
by Gill Scott Editions 2012
studio@gillscott-design.co.uk